# Bibliography for Beginners

# BIBLIOGRAPHY FOR BEGINNERS

SECOND EDITION

## DANIEL GORE

Macalester College

New York
APPLETON-CENTURY-CROFTS
Educational Division
MEREDITH CORPORATION

Copyright©1973 by

MEREDITH CORPORATION

All rights reserved

73 74 75 76 77/10 9 8 7 6 5 4 3 2 1

Library of Congress Card Number: 73-3860

Copyright©1968 by
Meredith Corporation under the title
*Bibliography For Beginners Form A*

Copyright©1966 by Daniel Gore under the title
*A Beginner's Book of Bibliography*

PRINTED IN THE UNITED STATES OF AMERICA

390-C-37660-4

Library of Congress Cataloging in Publication Data

Gore, Daniel.
    Bibliography for beginners: second edition.

    Published in 1966 under title: A beginner's book
of bibliography.
    Includes bibliographical references.
    1. Bibliography—Theory, methods, etc. I. Title.
Z1001.G6    1973        010'.1        73-3860
ISBN  0-390-37660-4

## TO THE MEMORY OF EDWARD MEYERS

His life was gentle, and the elements
So mix'd in him that Nature might stand up
And say to all the world, "This was a man!"

# Contents

*vii*

*Exercise*

# A Word to the Instructor

This book has been written with two slightly different courses in mind. The longer, probably three semester hours, would include the writing of a full-length research paper as the natural culmination of a course in practical bibliography, and the instructor might therefore wish to supplement this text with one of the standard writer's manuals. The shorter (one or two semester-hour) course would exclude the writing of a research paper, since the student would be bibliographically prepared to undertake that task in various other courses. I favor the longer course, since it keeps before the student a demanding goal that is not immediately present in the shorter one. But I have taught some twenty sections of the shorter course at the University of North Carolina at Asheville with satisfactory results, and do not doubt that others elsewhere can do as well, or better, with it.

Before setting your students to work on any of the exercises, you would do well to work through them yourself, to determine which (if any) of the problems cannot be solved in your library because the necessary books are missing from your collection. Since the problems were devised in a library with a small collection, however, you will probably find that most of them can be solved in your library.

If it is possible, you should review each student's work with him personally as he progresses through the exercises; otherwise, he is likely to perform them in such a perfunctory manner that he fails to perceive the principles underlying the work he has done. A few strategic questions in the course of a conference can be very effective in preventing this kind of lapse.

If more than about a hundred students are taking the course at the same time, and your library is a small one, it may be necessary for some sections to work on one set of assignments while other sections are working on some other assignments, to avoid undue congestion at the catalog and in the reference collection. The problem may not arise at all in large libraries. The normal sequence of assignments is 1-2-3-4-5-6-7-8-9-10-11, but thest two variants should also be satisfactory: 1-7-8-9-2-3-4-5-6-10-11; or, 1-5-6-7-8-9-2-3-4-10-11. With these three sequences being used simultaneously, crowding at the catalog of even a small library should never become so severe as to arouse in anyone a feeling less pleasant than that of normal human fellowship.

Any of the assignments may, of course, be reduced in length if need be;

as they now stand (omitting the term paper), most students will be able to complete them in less than fifty hours. Special circumstances in the local library may require complete revision of one or more of the assignments, but there should be no particular difficulty in devising alternatives that will illustrate the underlying principles as well as the originals were intended to do.

You will note that where the form of the assignment is determined by the classification sequence involved (Exercises 5.1, 5.11, 6.1, 6.11, 6.2, 6.21, 6.4, 6.41, 6.5, 6.51), the basic assignment is given in two forms: one for use in libraries classified by the Library of Congress system, the other for libraries classified by Dewey. For the rare library using neither of these, it should not be especially difficult to rearrange the order of questions to match the local classification sequence.

# A Word to the Student

The object of this little book is to introduce you in the simplest possible manner to a few prominent aspects of an extremely complicated subject: the history and organization of the world of books, the means of access to them, and the formal principles of describing them once you have found them. The topics that have been selected for discussion are those that seem to be of paramount importance to a student who will, perhaps for the first time in his life, be making a serious attempt to find his way around in the wilderness of books. By charting for you some of the broader pathways that have been cut through this seemingly impenetrable wilderness, we hope that later on you will be able to find your way alone down the numerous bypaths. For this reason, the book attempts to be neither comprehensive in its coverage nor exhaustive (or exhausting) in its treatment. It may sometimes leave you stuck fast in a thorn-thicket, but your instructor (or a librarian) should always be around to pry you loose.

A word about that strange word *bibliography:* it is neither spelled nor pronounced like *biography,* and its meaning is altogether different. It may be used in two senses—one, to mean the study of books; that is, the study of books as artifacts, as tangible physical objects, not exclusively as intellectual products. And in its other sense, the word, when accompanied by an article *(a* bibliography), means simply a list of writings. A list of books, newspapers, magazines, manuscripts—of anything that has been written or printed—is called a bibliography. It is therefore possible to make a bibliography of biographies, but a biography of bibliographies is out of the question.

This book is in two sections: the first begins with an essay on historical bibliography, followed by nine essays on the various principles to apply in trying to locate information and describe its source; the second section consists of practical exercises intended to bring into focus your understanding of typical problems in bibliography and their solutions. Before starting work on any of the exercises, read *carefully* both the essay that relates to it and the specific directions given as a headnote on the exercise sheet itself. Unless you understand perfectly what you are to do in each exercise, you are liable to waste much time that you could have spent better in playing tennis or chess, hiking, dating, or reading books. You should always be conscious that the intent of the assignment is, in most cases, to clarify for you the principle underlying the problem at hand. A clumsy solution may be worse than no solution at all, for at least in the latter case you may be impelled to correct a misunderstanding of principle that has led to the negative result.

When you have read this book and completed the exercises in it, you will still not be an expert bibliographer. But you will know enough about the use of libraries to begin to experience some of the pleasurable excitement that mature readers find in using good libraries properly. Libraries are full of hidden treasure. A lifetime is too short to find it all, a minute too long to waste in going about the search the wrong way.

# Acknowledgments

O. B. Hardison, Jr., Director of the Folger Shakespeare Library, read this book in manuscript and caught various lapses that have since been corrected. For his careful labor and timely assistance along the way, I am deeply indebted. One of my former teachers, Professor J. Penrose Harland of the Department of Classics, University of North Carolina at Chapel Hill, offered many valuable suggestions to improve the first chapter, for which I am most grateful. My former colleague, Dr. William Thurman of the University of North Carolina at Asheville, gave frequent and much appreciated aid in translating Greek and Latin passages when my own "small Latine and lesse Greeke" let me down. I owe special and innumerable debts to several hundred of my former students who helped me discover faults in earlier, experimental versions of the text. They will take satisfaction, I hope, in knowing their successors will be spared the problems they themselves so cheerfully endured. Those defects that remain are solely the author's responsibility since he has on occasion, when his advisers counseled another way, stubbornly followed his own.

For typing numerous preliminary versions of this book while carrying out their already heavy library duties, I am grateful to Mrs. Gladys Culbertson, Mrs. Annette Whitt, and Mrs. Sandra Kilpatrick, of the Library staff of the University of North Carolina at Asheville.

Finally, I wish to express particular thanks to Mrs. Jean Archibald, Associate Director of the Macalester College Library, for the expert help she gave in preparing the chapter on government documents; to my secretary, Mrs. Dorothy Barnes, for typing the manuscript, and to Miss Claudia Schorrig, for advice on matters of style.

D.G.

What Thoreau got, specifically, from Harvard was something quite indispensable. He was disciplined in the exactness, the accuracy, and the care for meaning which is the essence of scholarship. And, more important still, he learned to use a library.

Henry Seidel Canby, *Thoreau*

# I

# PRINCIPLES

# 1

# The History of Writing
# and the Making of Books

Who can say now—tens of thousands of years after the event—whether our great primal forefather, on beholding the sun and being moved to express his response to it in some fashion, was prompted to make a specific sound which he would thereafter associate with the object that had evoked it, or to draw a picture of the sun? If the initial impulse was to draw, rather than to make a noise, then writing predates speech.[1]

Whatever the order of priority was, and whatever the impulse that first prompted man either to write or to speak (some cynical linguists have proposed that speech arose from the compelling need to tell lies), it is perfectly clear that in the beginning, even if there was a Word (as St. John tells us), the first *writers* were not concerned with it, for they used pictures or written symbols to express not words, but things and ideas directly. And thousands of years were to pass before the truly amazing discovery was made that these written symbols could be used to represent not only objects and ideas directly but to represent the elemental sounds of a spoken language as well. That is, a visual symbol could be employed to represent an auditory symbol, which in turn could be used to represent (or misrepresent) a man's perceptions, thoughts, and feelings about his experience.

Cave drawings—some of them tens of thousands of years old—are commonly said to represent the first stage in the development of writing,

[1] No one knows just when the art of writing first arose, or even whether this art predates the origin of the human capacity to communicate by means of speech. If by "writing" one understands a visible record, in more or less permanent form, of the sounds of a spoken language, then the art of writing must necessarily come later than the faculty of speech. But if by "writing" one understands simply a visible record of perception, thought, or feeling, without regard to spoken language, then writing in this sense could have originated at any time before the origin of speech as well as after it. And the fact is that the first writing we know anything about had nothing whatever to do with language.

on the reasonable assumption that these drawings were intended by the artist to communicate something (precisely what is not known) either to himself or to other men. But the consummate artistry of many of these cave drawings[2] suggests a long stage of development, which at its beginning may have involved the use of much simpler drawings for purposes of communication: i.e., the use of drawing for utilitarian purposes (communication of fact) may have preceded its use for artistic purposes (the expression of feeling). At any rate, the utilitarian use of written symbols resulted in a set of drawings that were highly simplified—presumably to facilitate the rapid writing of them—and these written symbols are known as pictograms and ideograms. A pictogram is a very simple drawing of an object, whereas an ideogram is a pictorial expression of an idea. Pictographic systems of writing have been worked out independently by various groups of ancient men who, so far as we know, did not transmit their art from one group to another. Even so, it is no surprise that the pictograms for a particular object are often quite similar in the writing systems of widely separated people, since the form of the pictogram is originally determined by the natural object it represents. The pictograms for fish (not the *word,* but the thing itself), are quite similar in the North American Indian, ancient Chinese, Egyptian, and Babylonian pictographic systems.

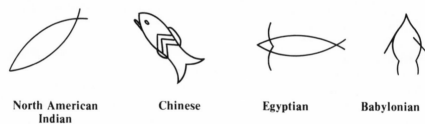

**North American Indian**          **Chinese**          **Egyptian**          **Babylonian**

The use of ideograms to express ideas, qualities, actions—anything that is not solid and static—must have posed some formidable problems to early writers, for there is no natural and inevitable correspondence between such things and pictorial symbols, as there is in the case of pictograms. What written symbol would you choose, for example, to express the idea of happiness in such a way that another writer would immediately perceive that this was precisely the idea you intended to communicate? The solution to this problem is not so easy as the choice of a fish-like shape to represent a fish, but such problems were solved with a high degree of ingenuity by

[2] Consult your library's catalog under the subject heading "Cave-Drawings" for a list of books in which you may find reproductions of these remarkable drawings.

ancient writers, undoubtedly through a prior agreement among the literate community as to precisely what ideas would be represented by what symbols. In the Chinese language, which to the present day makes considerable use of the ideographic system, the idea of happiness is represented by an ideogram which consists of a conjunction of the pictograms for "wife" and "child," conveying not only the abstract idea of happiness but something of the way in which the Chinese regard maternal ties.

Picto-ideographic writing systems were capable of communicating an enormous range of thought and feeling, and were sufficiently successful in some parts of the ancient world to endure for several thousand years, in spite of the fact that far more efficient phonetic systems of writing were available. Ancient Egyptian hieroglyphic writing is essentially picto-ideographic, but some phonetic symbols (that is, symbols representing the *sounds* of a spoken language, rather than objects or ideas) have been found in hieroglyphic inscriptions dating at least as far back as 4000 B.C. The Egyptians, clearly, had the idea of phonetic writing long before they chose to make any extensive use of it.[3]

The essential feature of phonetic writing, as distinguished from picto-ideographic writing, is its use of written symbols to represent spoken sounds. Phonetic writing systems appear to have gone through three distinct stages of development: first, a single symbol was employed to represent an entire word (logographic writing); then a symbol was used to represent each syllable in a word (syllabic writing); and, finally, a single symbol was used to represent a single distinctive sound feature in the spoken language. This last is, of course, alphabetic writing, although the ideal one-sound-to-one-symbol correspondence has only been approached in the alphabet and will probably never be fully realized, in spite of the various movements in recent decades to reform the alphabet.

Since no recorded text has come down to us in which an ancient writer tells us just why he abandoned the picto-ideographic system in favor of the phonetic, we can only infer what the reasons for the change may have been. An obvious inference is that the phonetic system, with fewer symbols to be mastered, would be much easier to learn. Even assuming a logographic system, where a different symbol is required for each word in the language, the number of symbols would be much less than in an ideographic system, because the number of possible ideas must greatly exceed the individual word count in any language. A fully developed picto-ideographic system will employ picto-ideograms running into the tens of thousands, whereas a syllabary system—one syllable/one symbol—can be constructed with several hundred symbols (Babylonian cuneiform is an example of this more

---

[3] Falconer Madan, *Books in Manuscript: A Short Introduction to Their Study and Use* ("Books about Books"; London: K. Paul, Trench, Trübner & Co., 1893), p. 21.

economical system). An alphabetic system, as you know, can manage with only twenty-six symbols, and some of these symbols are redundant (two symbols for the same sound), while there are many sounds (especially vowels) in the spoken language for which no alphabetic symbol exists.

Whether the relative ease of using phonetic systems gave rise to their adoption is open to question, since in ancient times the art of writing was universally the exclusive possession of the priestly classes—and they were never eager to share any of their special powers with the laity.[4] In all probability, the ancient Egyptian priesthood deliberately avoided wholesale adoption of phonetic symbols in their hieroglyphic writing for the very reason that it would have been much easier for an outsider to learn a purely phonetic system of writing and thus dilute one of the priesthood's more important sources of power.

Another plausible explanation for the transition to phonetic writing systems lies in the impossibility of writing the names of persons picto-ideographically. And the object of much of the earliest writing that has come down to us was simply to record the material obligations (wine, meat, grain, labor) of thousands of persons to their rulers. In order to make a list of persons and their particular debts to the king, one must be able to specify not only the nature of the debts, which would not be too difficult in picto-ideographic writing, but also the names of the individuals. One cannot, in fact, write a proper name without attention to phonetics, since a name is essentially nothing but a particular sequence of sounds. Persons may be correctly identified by other means than their names (the Army today uses serial numbers, which are in fact ideograms, to identify soldiers, but always in association with their names); but the difficulties are great, and any writer confronted with the problem of associating a very long list of picto-ideograms with living persons would soon begin to associate these written symbols with those persons' names—that is, with spoken sounds. As soon as he began to associate picto-ideograms with sounds, he would already have begun the transition to phonetic writing.

Whatever the causes that led to the development of phonetic writing, they were a very long time taking effect. Picto-ideographic writing systems were widely employed in the ancient world for at least several thousand years before the transition to a phonetic writing system reached its logical conclusion in the development of the alphabet at some time around 1600 B.C. We do not know what man or men invented the alphabet, but the mind that did possessed as great a genius as the world has ever known, and that genius has more profoundly shaped the entire course of human civilization than has any other in the long struggle for human

---

[4] The sense of mystery that has always, until very recent times, been associated with the art of writing is nowhere so plainly revealed as in our two English words "grammar" and "glamour," which are historically only phonetic variants of the same word: there was indeed a time when grammar *was* glamorous.

enlightenment. The first alphabet was a Semitic invention (the name of the alphabet comes from the names of the first two letters of the Semitic alphabet: aleph and beth), but the question of which group of ancient Semites should be honored as its inventor has never been settled.[5]

The alphabet is unique. Wherever an alphabetic system of writing has been employed, that system has derived ultimately from the ancient Semitic alphabet, in spite of the fact that the letter shapes may no longer bear any apparent resemblance to their ancient originals. If you examine a page of the Hindu scriptures in the Devanagari script, of the Koran in the Arab Kufic script, of the Old Testament in the Hebraic, of the New Testament in the Greek, of the English Bible in Roman or Gothic type, and of the Communist Manifesto in the Cyrillic alphabet of the Russians, you will find it difficult to believe that most of the letter shapes you see have a common ancestor, so great and varied have their changes been over the course of hundreds of years. To be sure, each nation that has adopted the alphabet has made various minor adjustments in it according to requirements of its own language—the English alphabet added to the Roman alphabet the letter J to account for the distinction between the consonantal and vocalic I—but the fundamental invention of an alphabetical system of writing occurred only once, somewhere in the Near East, and was thereafter borrowed by many nations and applied to their own languages.

The most important modifications to the ancient Semitic alphabet were made by the Greeks, who received the alphabet, by way of the Phoenicians, sometime between the thirteenth century and the eighth century B.C. (the precise date has never been conclusively settled). The common belief of antiquity was that the art of alphabetic writing was brought to Greece from Tyre, an ancient Phoenician city, by Cadmus, a mythical hero whose real-life counterpart is conjectured to have lived around the thirteenth century B.C.[6] The date for the Greek reception of the alphabet that is most widely accepted by authorities today is the early ninth century B.C.[7] The Semitic origin of the Greek alphabet is, at any rate, unquestioned: the *names* of the letters of the Semitic alphabet were even taken over by the Greeks, although these names were meaningless in the

---

[5] The use of the term "alphabet" to describe the ancient Semitic system of writing is objected to by some paleographers on the ground that no provision was made in that system for indicating the vowel sounds. Only the consonants were provided for in the original twenty-two letter system, and to this day the Hebrew alphabet contains only consonants, despite various efforts to remedy this deficiency. But since the essence of alphabetic writing is the use of *one* written symbol to represent *one* sound—and it was the ancient Semites who first had the idea of using such a system, although they failed to perfect it (as have we)—the Semitic people may still be fairly credited with this marvelous invention.

[6] B. L. Ullman, *Ancient Writing and Its Influence* ("Our Debt to Greece and Rome"; New York: Cooper Square Publishers, 1963), pp. 21-22. Mr. Ullman's book was first published in 1932.

[7] Personal communication from Professor Penrose Harland.

Greek language. Thus *aleph* and *beth* in Hebrew mean, respectively, ox and house; but the names *alpha* and *beta* mean nothing in the Greek language.

The Greek people, always innovators, made two very important changes in the Semitic alphabet. First, they changed the direction in which the script was written. Semitic scripts to this day are written from the right edge of the page to the left; while the Greek script, and the scripts of other peoples who got their alphabet by way of the Greeks (the Romans, the English, the Russians, and others), are always written from left to right. The Greeks also experimented with two-directional writing, where alternate lines are written in opposite directions. This is called *boustrophedon* writing, meaning literally "ox-turn-like writing," since the direction of lines shifts in the pattern that would be made by an ox plowing a field. A passage of boustrophedon would look like this:

## WE REACH THE END OF A LINE

## AND OUR EYE DOUBLES BACK

## AND GOES THE OTHER WAY

## AND DOUBLES BACK AGAIN

Boustrophedon was finally abandoned by the Greeks in favor of one-directional, left-to-right writing, but no one knows just why they gave it up. On the surface, it appears to be the ideal system, since it saves a reader the eye shift that in one-directional writing is always required at the end of a line.

The second change the Greeks made in the Semitic alphabet, and by far the more important, was the adoption of certain letters for the vowel sounds in their language. The ancient Semitic alphabet was strictly consonantal: that is, letters were provided for the consonants only, and the reader was left to guess at the vowel sounds between them. In such a system, the word *"blackboard"* might simply be written *"blkbrd."* As you can imagine, such a system would lead to many ambiguities (for example, would *"btl"* be *"beetle," "battle,"* or *"bottle"?*), and the Greeks, perceiving this defect, adopted letters for five of the vowel sounds in their language. The reason they adopted only five, when the number of perceptible vowel sounds in Greek is much greater, was that there were only five redundant letters (that is, letters whose function was duplicated by another letter in the alphabet, as with our k and c), in the Semitic alphabet, and the Greeks could use them to represent vowels without going to the trouble of inventing new letter shapes to cover the other vowel sounds. This reduction to five vowel sounds was later accepted by the Romans, and eventually by the English, with the result that to this day our alphabet is woefully short on letters to represent vowels, forcing us to resort to numerous makeshifts.

The Romans received the alphabet from the Greeks, probably by way of the Etruscans, no later than 600 B.C., and to them largely belongs the credit for transmitting, during the years of the Empire, the art of alphabetic writing to most of the civilized nations of the earth. The other great contribution the Romans made to the alphabetic art was literally an artistic one: they perfected the shapes of the capital letters of the alphabet and, in doing so, virtually fixed their form for all time.

Of the origin of letter shapes little is known, and even that little is widely debated. The shape of the letter A, for example, is held by some to have been determined by the shape of the head of the animal for which it was named: the ox. Stand the letter A on its head (and in ancient scripts, letters may be found in almost any orientation, standing up, lying down, and upside down), place two dots in it for eyes (this for its suggestive value only), and the horned head of the ox is not at all difficult to see:

As noted above, the Semitic name for this letter is *aleph,* which means ox, and the first letter in that name is the letter A (in Semitic a consonant, not a vowel); so it seems reasonable to assume that the shape of the letter was determined by the name of a thing that had this letter as its initial. On the other hand, the letter shape itself may have been completely arbitrary and without a name at first; perhaps some later writer, perceiving its fortuitous resemblance to an ox's head, gave it the name *aleph.* Many other letters of the Semitic alphabet have no discernible connection between their shape and that of the thing for which they were named.

The shapes of the letters underwent many changes before reaching what we may now call the final and perfect form of the capitals in Rome in the second century A.D. Many examples of beautiful monumental lettering have come down to us from that time, but the most famous of all—the example that was to become a standard for letter design among calligraphers and type designers ever afterward—was an inscription at the base of Trajan's Column, erected in the year A.D. 113 in the Trajan Forum to commemorate the conquest of the Dacian people by the emperor Trajan.[8] The transcendent beauty of the letters in this inscription is immediately perceived by all who have seen them. Their amazing freshness and modernity of appearance, so untypical of any art form created nearly two thousand years ago, is accounted for by the simple fact that modern type designers have returned again and again to these ancient letters for

---

[8] Edward M. Catich, *Letters Redrawn from the Trajan Inscription in Rome* (2nd ed.; Davenport, Iowa: Catfish Press, 1961), pp. 1-6.

inspiration and correction in working out their own designs. (Several tracings of these letters, reduced in size, appear below). Persons who are unfamiliar with the calligraphic and typographical arts will have some difficulty at first in appreciating the enormous significance attached to these Trajan letters by historians of art. But a few moments' reflection leads to a realization that the art of lettering is indeed the art of arts; no other art form even approaches the powerful and pervasive influence exerted by the

**Tracings of letters from the Trajan Column, A.D. 113 (reduced). Note the distinct leftward tilt of the center line of the letter O. This feature has been faithfully copied by many type designers and letterers of monuments in our own century—1800 years after the letter was first designed by the unknown Trajan artist.**

art of lettering on human affairs. Certainly no other art has had anything like the universal application of the art of lettering, and it is in this art form alone that the Roman people not only excelled but were completely original. Their sculptures, buildings, poems, dramas, myths—all that we know anything about—were derived mainly from the Greeks and are generally held to be inferior to the artistic achievements of the Greeks. But in their monumental capital letters, the Romans are unrivalled. How appropriate that this nation of eminently practical men should excel only in this most practical of all the arts. The artist who designed the Trajan letters is completely unknown to us, although he may fairly be ranked with the greatest artistic talent the world has known. Like those powerful geniuses who created the Greek myths, he has left us only his work to marvel at; the insignificant facts of his mortal life he kept to himself.

To make these beautiful capital letters even on paper, with their gracefully swelling thick lines, delicate thins, and elegant serifs,[9] takes skill and patient labor, more than most men are willing to commit to the production of any but the most important writings. Roman business documents and Roman graffiti (scribblings on walls) were therefore not done in formal capitals like those on the Trajan Column, but the works of Vergil sometimes were, indicating something of the reverence Romans had for their greatest poet.

For their informal writings, the Romans used a script that could be written far more rapidly than the formal capitals, by virtue of the fact that serifs and delicate shadings of line were not used, and letters were connected, so that the pen would not have to be lifted from the page in moving from one letter to the next. This is called cursive writing, literally "running" writing, and is of course widely used today. While this style of writing was not used as a formal book-hand, the speed and carelessness of execution characteristic of the cursive hand led later to the development of some of the small letters used in the formal book-hand. But the Romans failed to develop a small-letter alphabet worthy of becoming, as did their Trajan capitals, a universal standard for letter shapes.

The Romans also used forms of the capital letters other than the "square" capitals derived from monument inscriptions. Of these, the uncial capitals, a rounded version of the square capitals, were widely used as a book-hand as late as the ninth century but failed in the long run to be accepted as a permanent standard. With the decline of Roman influence after the fifth century, various "national" book-hands, each using letter shapes markedly different from those of the other book-hands, developed in the several regions of Western Europe.

---

[9] You may have wondered why type designers usually put those little hooks, called serifs, as finishing strokes on letters. They do it simply because the artist of the Trajan letters did it and thereby added beauty to his work.

This Babel of book-hands persisted in Western Europe until the time of Charlemagne, who, as his political power grew toward the close of the eighth century, undertook to restore some of the cultural unity that had been lost with the fall of the western branch of the Roman Empire.

To the left, **Visigothic hand, written in Spain (enlarged)**. To the right, **Beneventan hand, written in Italy (enlarged)**.

**Merovingian hand, written in France (enlarged).**

One of the more important results of this ambition was the development of a standard book-hand, widely adopted by the scribes of Western Europe. It became, many centuries later, the model on which our printed lowercase letters were based. The small letters of this famous book-hand are known as Carolingian minuscules, which means quite simply, *"Charles's small letters.*"[10] Below you will see several specimens of the Carolingian minuscules and may recognize them as the remote ancestor of the small letters on the page you are now reading.

Like all living things, the Carolingian minuscules underwent gradual changes from generation to generation, the letters becoming more and more compressed to save valuable writing materials, heavier in line, and with pointed finishing strokes added, until by the thirteenth century an

**Carolingian minuscule, written in France, early ninth century (enlarged).**

[10] Charlemagne did not devise the letters himself, of course. He commanded that they be made, and they were made—by monks.

uirginitate mana
femper prole fecun
&caritatif uof mun
&fuae inuobif ben
na infundat ·  ⋏

Carolingian minuscule, written in England, tenth century (enlarged).

cum idem artifex deus · po
inomnem fabricam eidem
fuerat traditurus· Vt quem
prefidem poft fe facere dif
eundem faceret plenum ai
babentem infe et dignitate

Carolingian minuscule, written in Italy, early twelfth century (enlarged).

essentially new book-hand had evolved directly out of the Carolingian miniscule. This new hand (see below) later came to be called "Gothic" by Renaissance scholars, although the barbarian Goths had not the slightest connection with it. The term "Gothic" was simply applied to it by the

ti lac dedit; et in phiala principū
obtulit butirum; Sinistrā ma
num misit ad claudum; et dex
teram ad fabrorū malleos; Per
cussit cp̄ sisaram; querens in ca
pite uulneri locum; ⁊ timp̄ uali
de pforans; Inter pedes eius ruit;
defecit et mortuus est; Ante pedes
eius uoluebatur; et iacebat exani
mis ⁊ miserabilis; Per fenestrā
pspiciens ululabat mater eius
⁊ de cenaculo loquebatur; Cur
morantur regredi currus eius?
Quare tardauerunt pedes qua

**Gothic hand (full-scale), from a manuscript Bible, thirteenth or fourteenth century (Chapter 4, Judges).**

bus : cuam mobili in me mcosq̃ cñe animo non sperabam . Me interea nec do mesticus dolor . nec cinusq̃ iniuria ab re p. abducet .

ARCVS TVLLIVS . M . FI . CICERO . Q. metello . Q. fi . celeri pro conf sat . p. d . . Si tu exercitusq̃ ualens bene est . Scribis ad me te ex istimasse pro mutuo inter nos animo et pro reconciliata gratia nū et a me ludibrio lesum in . Quod cuiusmodi sit : satis intelligere non possu. Sed tamen suspicor ad te cñe allatum me in senatum quom disputarem per multos cñe : qui rem p a me conseruatam dolerent . dixisse a te propinquos t tuos quibus negare non potuisset impetrasse . Vt ca que statuisset tibi in sena

**Humanistic hand, from a fifteenth-century manuscript.**

humanists as an expression of their contempt for all things medieval. Unfortunately, the appellation has stuck, to the confusion of students, who naturally assume that Gothic writing must have been written by the Goths, and to the abiding irritation of medievalists and paleographers, who are fully conscious that the Gothic hand, far from being contemptible, is one of the liveliest and loveliest of all book-hands.

The use of the Gothic book-hand persisted throughout Western Europe right down to the invention of printing, with one important exception. In Italy, at the beginning of the Renaissance in the fifteenth century, a new book-hand known as the humanistic script was developed by Greek and Latin scholars who, in searching for classical texts generally forgotten in the later Middle Ages, came upon the ancient manuscripts of the ninth, tenth, and eleventh centuries written in the Carolingian hand. Because they found so many of the neglected classical texts written in this hand, they naturally came to look upon it as the "classical" hand, and chose it as a model for their own book-hands in preference to the hands of more recent centuries, which they associated with religious texts of the later Middle Ages. The humanistic script, a revival with some modifications of the ancient Carolingian hand, is the last stage in the development of the great book-hands. After the invention in the fifteenth century of the art of printing from movable types, book-hands survived as potent influences on the design of metal types to be used in the mechanical production of books.

## THE MATERIALS AND IMPLEMENTS FOR WRITING

As a child will attempt his first writing on surfaces that are most conveniently available to him, early man chose to write on materials that required little or no preparation: the walls of caves, the rock face of a cliff, pieces of wood, hides of animals. Much later, the surface of a cliff might be planed smooth for the incision of a monumental inscription, such as the gigantic testament to himself left by Darius the Great on the cliff of Behistun. A huge slab of stone might be dressed and inscribed to produce such monuments as the Egyptian obelisks; or hides of animals might be split, tanned, and carefully dressed to make the splendid writing material we now call parchment.

The most commonly used writing materials of the ancient world were clay tablets (often baked, but not always), papyrus, and, for monumental inscriptions, stone. Clay tablets were the favorite writing material of the Babylonian scribes made impressions in the wet clay with a wedge-shaped quantity, would take a clear impression when wet, and was practically indestructible when dry, even if unbaked. Thousands of these tablets, after lying buried in the moist ground for thousands of years, have recently been dug up, dried out, brushed clean, and baked, making them as fine and clean as they were on the day when some ancient scribe wrote on them.[11] Babylonians scribes made impressions in the wet clay with a wedge-shaped stylus (whence our word "style"), and the script they used (a syllabary) has come to be called cuneiform, from the Latin word *cuneus,* a wedge.

Papyrus was the preferred writing material of the Egyptians, because the papyrus plant grew in great abundance in the region of the Nile and could, with relative ease, be made into a suitable writing surface. The marrow of the plant was slit into thin strips that were then arranged in two layers at right angles to each other, perhaps treated with a gum solution, and pounded together to form a sheet for writing. Its use in Egypt as a writing material is ancient, and the bulk of the earliest Greek and Latin manuscripts that have come down to us are made of papyrus. The people of North Africa exported large quantities of papyrus to Greece and Rome. As a result of this export business we have today our words "Bible" and "bibliography" (it was from the ancient Syrian city of Byblos that the Greeks obtained their papyrus). The Greeks at first called the papyrus strips βυβλοι ("the stuff from Byblos") and then the books made from it βιβλοι, a word that later entered the Latin language as *biblia* and the English language as "Bible."

Although it later gave way to parchment, papyrus continued to be used as a writing material right down to the eleventh century A.D., in spite of the fact that, of all possible materials for *permanent* record, papyrus was one of the worst. Even when it was fresh and first written upon, great care was required to avoid damaging the papyrus sheet. For this reason, a brush-like pen was used, and the strokes made with it were always light. As it dried out with age, papyrus became as brittle as fallen leaves in winter; thus, any papyrus sheet that you see today will be enclosed by two panes of glass, to prevent its disintegration.[12]

[11] Edward Chiera, *They Wrote on Clay: The Babylonian Tablets Speak Today,* ed. George G. Cameron (Chicago: The University of Chicago Press, 1964, c1938), pp. 17-22.

[12] Madan, pp. 6-9.

The finest of all commonly used writing materials is parchment, the carefully prepared skin of animals, principally sheep and goats, and its deluxe version, vellum, made from the skin of calves. In durability it surpasses all but the monumental materials such as stone, and the excessively bulky clay tablets of the Babylonians. As a surface for the reception of writing, it has no rival; any stroke the calligrapher may wish to apply with a wooden, quill, or metal pen is readily received by the smooth but tough surface. A calligrapher can thus pursue a variety of artistic ends, a circumstance of considerable consequence to medieval scribes as they began to explore the possibilities of Carolingian and Gothic hands.

The development of parchment is attributed to Eumenes II, who ruled over the little Greek kingdom of Pergamum in Asia Minor in the first half of the second century B.C. and aspired to build a royal library that would surpass even the great Egyptian library in Alexandria. Jealous, perhaps, of Eumenes's ambition to outstrip the Egyptian national library, the Ptolemies severely limited the export of papyrus to Pergamum, compelling Eumenes to find some equally suitable writing material. The result of this adversity was the production of parchment, named for the place in which it was first made.[13] "Pergamum" becomes "parchment" through phonetic changes similar to those which caused "vermin" to become "varmint."

By the first century A.D. parchment could easily be obtained in Rome, and by the fourth century it had taken the place of papyrus as the most widely used writing material.[14] It was during this same period that the codex, or leaf, form of the book came into general use; it eventually displaced the ancient scroll form, just as parchment displaced papyrus, although both forms remained in simultaneous use for many years. The scroll form, of great antiquity, was virtually necessitated by the use of papyrus as a writing material, since its fragility was such that individual sheets could not possibly be stitched or otherwise bound together. The only way to keep the sheets of a papyrus book safely together was to glue them together edge to edge, producing a very long sheet that had then to be rolled up for convenient storage and use. (Our word "volume," incidentally, comes from the Latin *volvo*, "roll," which the Romans applied in its substantive form *volumen* to the scroll form of the book.) The scroll has one serious defect from the standpoint of use that is immediately apparent to anyone who has ever read one. When the end of the book is reached, it must be rolled the other way before it can be read again; and if one wishes to consult a single page of the text, instead of turning directly to it as in the leaf form of the book, one must unroll the scroll to the page one wants and then roll it back up again. The codex book does not cause such inconvenience but such a book can be made only if the writing is done on

[13] *Ibid.,* pp. 9-10.
[14] James Hayes, *The Roman Letter* ... (Chicago: Donnelly, [1952?]), p. 8.

leaves that are made of material stout enough for the leaves to be stitched along their inner margins to form a permanent binding. Parchment and, much later, paper, both perfectly suited to this treatment, made possible a great technological improvement which had been impossible with papyrus. Mere technical improvement, however, has often failed in the past to win men over immediately. But in this instance the attitude of the early Christian church toward the ancient scroll had a lot to do with making the new codex form popular. The scroll was naturally associated by the church fathers with the pagan literature transmitted by these scrolls, and they felt the newer, untainted codex form was more appropriate for transmission of Christian writings.[15] Their choice of the codex form was at least as good on purely utilitarian grounds as it was on theological ones. The joint result was that the codex form became nearly universal in the Middle Ages, and persists to the present day as the best conceivable form of the book. Perhaps other forms will eventually supplant the codex, but no form even remotely approaching it in ease of use has been proposed during the two thousand years it has been in existence.

The displacement of parchment by paper as the common writing material of Western Europe occurred more than a thousand years after the invention of paper in China (A.D. 105), and about three centuries after the establishment of the first paper mill in Europe by the Moors in Xativa, Spain (ca. 1150). Indeed, the use of paper for making books was not generally accepted until the enormous demands of the printing press—beginning in the 1450s, the decade of the printing of the Gutenberg Bible—overwhelmed the capacity of the parchmenters to supply their product. It is estimated that the thirty-odd copies of Gutenberg's Bible which were printed on vellum required the skins of at least 5,000 calves.[16] If the entire edition had been printed on vellum (some 150 copies were printed on paper),[17] this one book would have led to the slaughter of some 30,000 calves. Given the thousands of other books printed in Western Europe before the end of the fifteenth century, the sheep and the cow would shortly have become extinct had not printers adopted a substitute for vellum and parchment.

One of the reasons for reluctance to accept paper as a substitute for parchment and vellum has come down to us in the words of Abbot Johann Tritheim: "Truly if writing is set down on vellum, it will last for a millennium. When printing is on paper, however, how long will it last? It would be much if printing in a paper volume were to survive for two

---

[15] Douglas C. McMurtrie, *The Book: The Story of Printing & Bookmaking* (3rd rev. ed.; New York: Oxford University Press, 1962, c1943), p. 76.

[16] Curt F. Bühler, *The Fifteenth Century Book: The Scribes, the Printers, the Decorators* ("Publications of the A. S. W. Rosenbach Fellowship in Bibliography"; Philadelphia: University of Pennsylvania Press, 1961), p. 42.

[17] *Ibid.,* p. 53.

hundred years."[18] But despite its relative fragility in comparison with parchment and the fact that it was not so beautiful a writing surface as fine vellum, paper had the virtues of cheapness and limitless supply that parchment lacked. These virtues were decisive, of course, once the printing press made possible the rapid production of books in any quantity desired. And, notwithstanding the reasonable doubts of Abbot Johann, paper made of linen rags—as most paper was until about a hundred years ago—could, if stored properly, last forever. We have today innumerable examples of paper in excellent condition—tough, resilient, and unspoiled by discoloration—even though they were made five hundred years ago. Since the latter part of the nineteenth century, rag paper has largely been supplanted by paper made from wood pulp. But chemicals used in making pulp paper cause it to discolor and disintegrate quite rapidly, with the result that much of the contents of modern libraries will not survive to the next century. Very recent improvements in the chemical treatment of wood pulp now make possible production of wood-pulp paper with lasting qualities apparently as good as those of rag paper. Pulp-paper books made hereafter may last as long as those produced in the fifteenth century if this forecast does not prove to be as overly optimistic as Abbot Johann's was pessimistic.

## THE MEDIEVAL BOOK (ca. A.D. 800–1450)[19]

Whatever has come down to us from the vast body of classical Greek and Roman literature has survived through the labors of thousands of scribes, patiently copying (and sometimes miscopying) by hand the texts that each succeeding generation thought worthy of preservation. Obvious though it is, we sometimes lose sight of the fact that until about the year 1440, *every document and every book was written by hand.* Some classical texts, for example those of Tacitus and Catullus, came perilously close to being lost to us forever. They have survived in a single manuscript copy, as does the text of the Old English epic poem *Beowulf.* This masterpiece was nearly destroyed by a fire that burnt away its margins; had several inches more been consumed, we would have no record whatever of this now famous poem. To the everlasting regret of historians and classical scholars, this method of transmitting ancient literature by hand-copying undoubtedly resulted in the loss of far more texts than were preserved. Our entire heritage of complete classical texts amounts to no more than five or six hundred titles. (The annual production of new books today in the United States alone is in the range of twenty thousand titles). But quite probably the

---

[18] Quoted in Bühler, p. 35.
[19] The facts for the discussion which follows are largely derived from Madan's *Books in Manuscript,* chapters 4 through 6.

number of titles produced during a number of centuries in classical Greece and Rome numbered in the hundreds of thousands; hence, about one book in a thousand has survived the winnowing process of time and scribal selection.

On those texts that the medieval bookmaker thought worthy of preservation and duplication, he often bestowed artistic powers of the very highest order, with the result that many of the medieval books can be ranked fairly with the artistic productions (especially paintings) of any age or place. Besides the art of lettering (calligraphy), which had been brought to perfection in the Carolingian and Gothic hands, the art of painting and of decoration was widely exercised in the production of manuscript books. Initial letters, ranging in height from a half-inch to as much as ten inches, would often have painted within them portraits or religious scenes done in amazing detail and with consummate artistry. These paintings within the borders of initial letters came to be called miniatures, from the Latin word *miniare,* "to paint red," a color often used by the medieval artist. And because of the typically diminutive size of the paintings, the word "miniature" later came to be applied to other small scale paintings or sculptures. Besides miniatures, a page will often have wide borders lavishly decorated, or illuminated (to use the technical term): leafy branches grow out of the edge of an initial letter at the margin; birds and butterflies range among the leaves and branches; and sometimes grotesque animals twine about the branches and each other, as if in leering mockery of man's vaunted capacity to make books. The sumptuousness of some of these manuscript pages beggars description: a sheet of fine vellum may be dyed a deep purple and then have a text written upon it in letters of real gold, or of silver, carefully burnished to produce an effect of almost Oriental splendor.

No photographic reproductions of pages from these remarkable books can represent adequately their startling beauty. Better to see nothing at all than to receive the mistaken impressions that reproductions always give of the character of this art. Since literally thousands of these pages, either loose or still in their original bindings, have come down to us, anyone who wishes may conveniently see one if he lives near a university library (most of them have various examples of medieval book art) or a museum that exhibits art of the Middle Ages. The reverence our ancestors had for the written word can be understood best by beholding directly the striking pages of books written centuries ago by men who wished to glorify God in the beauty of their own creations.

Most of the book production in the Middle Ages was, of course, carried on in monasteries, but nothing prevented anyone from making his own book by simply copying out the text from another work. Many such manuscripts, most of them of no artistic merit, have survived. The monastic scribes, highly skilled and severely disciplined in their art, worked in a section of the monastery called the *scriptorium.* From some of their colophons (a paragraph at the end of a book telling when and where it is copied) we know the scribes sometimes found the work of copying day after day extremely wearisome. The following excerpts from medieval colophons express some of the emotions felt by a scribe when he reached the end of his task:

*Finito libro reddatur gratia Christo.*
"With the book completed, may thanks be given to Christ."
*Finito libro frangamus ossa magistro.*
"Now the book is finished, let's break our master's bones."
*Finis succrevit, manus et mea fessa quievit.*
"The work is finished, and my weary hand has found rest."
*Nunc scripsi totum; pro Christo da mihi potum.*
"Now I've written it all: for Christ's sake give me a drink."
*Vinum scriptori debetur de meliori.*
"The scribe deserves the very best wine."

Any task requiring such sustained and painstaking attention as the copying of a book opens the way to numerous errors, for the presence of which the scribes would sometimes make quite unashamed apologies as in the two following examples:

*Qui leget emendat, scriptorem non reprehendat.*
"Let him who reads correct the errors, and not blame the scribe."
*Si erravit scriptor, debes corrigere, lector.*
"If the scribe has erred, then you must make the corrections, gentle reader."

The feeling of ancient authors about scribal infidelities is vividly expressed in the concluding verses of the Bible (Revelation 22:18-19), which are directly aimed at the careless (or dishonest) scribe:

For I testify unto every man that heareth the words of the prophecy of this book, if any man shall add unto these things, God shall add unto him the plagues that are written in this book:

And if any man shall take away from the words of the book of this prophecy, God shall take away his part out of the book of life, and out of the holy city, and from the things which are written in this book.

Another well-known thrust at the careless scribe is that with which the bishop Irenaeus concluded a book against heretics ("On the Ogdoad"):

I adjure thee, who shalt copy out of this book, by our Lord Jesus Christ, by his glorious advent when he comes to judge the living and the dead, that thou compare what thou shalt transcribe and correct it with this copy whence thou art transcribing, with all care, and thou shalt likewise transcribe this oath and put it in the copy.

These closing lines were transcribed and thus preserved in Eusebius's *Ecclesiastical History,* V, xx, 2-6; ironically, they are about the only portion of Irenaeus's whole book that has survived.

One of the more fruitful endeavors of modern scholarship has been the rectification of scribal blunders through the close analysis of known errors, which reveals the type of error that is likely to be made, thus providing a basis for inference in the case of suspected blunders; and through the comparison of related texts known to have derived from a common source, in order to determine the probable authentic version (now lost) of a passage suspected to be corrupt.

It may be imagined that, with Western Europe suddenly flooded with printed books after the 1460s, the expensive production of manuscript books would have ceased with equal suddenness, throwing all of the scribes into technological unemployment. But this was not at all the case. For, as Curt Bühler tells us, "nearly as many manuscripts written in the second half of the fifteenth century have come down to us as those which are judged to belong to the first half-century. Further, it seems most improbable that the proportional relationship between what was written and what has survived would differ materially for these closely related periods."[20] The continuing demand for handwritten books even after Gutenberg's time may be conjecturally explained on various grounds, not the least of which was their supreme beauty, which continued to attract buyers who appreciated books as artifacts and could afford to indulge this appreciation. Also, texts in Greek still had to be copied by hand until the very end of the fifteenth century, since no suitable metal types had yet been produced for the Greek alphabet. And if anyone wanted a copy of a book that no printer had yet dared or thought desirable enough to print, it could be obtained only in manuscript form.

## THE FIFTEENTH-CENTURY BOOK

The printed books of the fifteenth century (called nowadays *incunabula,* a Latin word meaning cradle, birthplace, childhood, a beginning) bore, in fact, many close resemblances to the manuscript books that immediately preceded them and existed simultaneously with them until the end of the century. For one thing, the letter shapes used in the typographical book were directly based on the letter shapes then being used in the manuscript books, since those were the only reasonable models for the type designer to follow. The illustrations below of a thirteenth century manuscript Bible leaf and a leaf from Gutenberg's printed Bible (ca. 1456) exhibit plainly the influence of contemporary calligraphy on the typography of the time. But printers of incunabula even went beyond imitating typefaces to make their

---

[20] Bühler, *The Fifteenth Century Book,* p. 25.

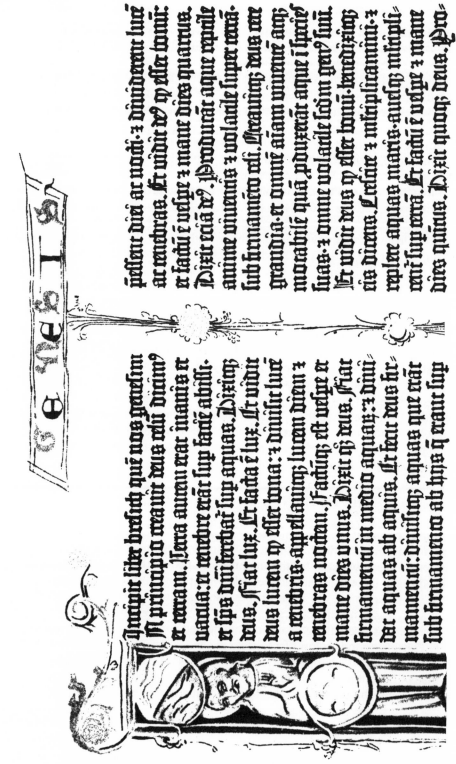

Portion of a page from the Gutenberg Bible, ca. 1456 (slightly reduced).

printed books resemble manuscript books. They would often leave large square blank spaces at the beginning of a major section in the text so that, once the page was printed, an illuminator could fill up the blank space with a richly decorated initial letter, just as makers of manuscript books had done. And the borders of a printed page, like the Gutenberg page opposite, would sometimes be illuminated by hand with the same elaboration of color and design employed on the borders of manuscript books. The intent of the printers obviously was to make the transition from the old and revered to the new and untrusted form as easy as possible for prospective purchasers, who could, if they chose, have mechanically printed books made to be almost indistinguishable from the handwritten books they were accustomed to reading.

Portion of a page from a manuscript Bible written in the Gothic hand around the thirteenth century (slightly reduced).

Appreciation for Gutenberg's famous invention of printing from movable types increases greatly when one realizes that he had not only to solve the enormously difficult technological problems of printing from cast metal types (this took him at least some ten or fifteen years), but to bring that radically new technology to a state of near perfection right at the beginning, in order to produce a book that would be a suitable rival to the wondrously beautiful handmade books of the Middle Ages. Nothing in the history of technology quite rivals Gutenberg's achievement. One would expect the first major products from this new invention to exhibit all the crudities commonly associated with pioneer efforts; yet in the entire history of printing since Gutenberg's time only a handful of printed books equals or even approaches the awesome beauty of Gutenberg's noble Bible.

Little is known about the long period of experimentation that led to the printing of the Bible, in spite of many years of patient research by hundreds of scholars; and the few solid facts that have come down to us lead to deductions that are debatable.[21] Scholars generally agree that Gutenberg was driven out of the printing business, and into bankruptcy, by his partners Johann Fust and Peter Schöffer. His expulsion occurred either before or shortly after the actual printing of the so-called Gutenberg Bible got under way, so we may fairly say, ironically enough, that Gutenberg was not the printer of the Gutenberg Bible.

The appearance of printed books just at the crucial moment of the Renaissance, when a sudden outburst of creative and scholarly energy in Western Europe led to vast demands for the instruments of learning, can hardly have been fortuitous. A new and momentous demand for books had grown out of the rediscovery of the long-neglected philosophical and literary monuments of the pagan past, and a means was soon found for supplying that demand: the printing press. The art of printing from movable types soon spread outward from the city of Mainz, where Gutenberg had perfected it, to all the countries of Western Europe. In 1467 two German printers from Mainz, Sweynheim and Pannartz, established themselves in Rome and printed the first book in a style subsequently called Roman. Unlike Gutenberg, who had based his type designs on the Gothic hand then, with the exception of Italy, universally employed in manuscript books, Sweynheim and Pannartz designed types after the letter shapes used in the humanistic hand, which was based on the Carolingian minuscule.[22] The reason for this choice is obvious: Italian humanists disdained the Gothic hand. As a result of their choice, which was later imitated throughout Italy and, much later, throughout Western Europe (with the single major exception of Germany, which retained the Gothic type until the twentieth century), the letters you are now reading are printed in one of the many later variants of this original Roman type.

The third great genus of typeface—the italic—appeared right at the close of the incunabula period. In the year 1500, the great Venetian printer Aldus Manutius had one of his typemakers design a font modeled on a book-hand called chancery after the Vatican chancery, where it was developed, and employed in correspondence and transcription of minor

---

[21] For an excellent survey of this problem, see chapters 10 and 11 of McMurtrie's *The Book* (cited above).

[22] Daniel Berkeley Updike, *Printing Types: Their History, Forms, and Use: A Study in Survivals* (2 vols., 3rd ed.; Cambridge: The Belknap Press of Harvard University Press, 1962), I, 71-72. Mr. Updike's book contains many excellent facsimiles of printed texts, illustrating the evolution of type designs from the incunabula period to the nineteenth century.

documents.[23] All subsequent typefaces that have been widely used are merely the individual expression of some type designer's response to the three great fifteenth-century models: the Gothic, the Roman, and the italic, which in turn were simply translations into metallic type of the Gothic, humanistic, and chancery book-hands. All three have a common ancestor in the great Carolingian minuscle (ca. A.D. 800); the latter two, in their capital letters, have a common ancestor in the famous letters incised on the base of the Trajan Column in the year A.D. 113.

Of the many other important figures in the history of typography, two may be singled out for brief mention here as being of particular interest to American readers: William Caxton, who printed the first book in the English language, and Stephen Daye, the first printer in the American colonies. Caxton's book, the *Recuyell of the Histories of Troye,* was printed not in England, but in the city of Bruges, on the Continent, where he was for a time "governor" of the English Merchant Adventurers resident in the city. The publication date was sometime between 1474 and 1476, and the typeface used by Caxton was a singularly wiry, nervous, and ugly variety of Gothic which seems almost illegible to us today. Shortly after publication of this book, Caxton returned to England and established a printing shop in the Almonry, near Westminster Abbey, which after his death in 1491 was operated by his foreman Wynkyn de Worde.[24]

The first colonial press was set up in Cambridge, Massachusetts, by the locksmith Stephen Daye and his son Matthew, who already had some experience as a printer. The first fruit of their press, and hence the first piece of colonial printing, was a broadside halfsheet entitled "The Freeman's Oath," no copy of which is known to have survived.[25] Like Caxton's work, Daye's has no esthetic distinction whatever, but the historical interest that attaches to it is of course considerable by virtue of his priority in this most powerful of the civilizing arts.

Since the days of the incunabula, many technological improvements in the art of printing have made possible the far more rapid production of books. But with few exceptions, printed books of the seventeeth and later centuries are far less beautiful than those of the fifteenth and sixteenth. The temptation to blame this inferiority on exploitation of mass production techniques for purely economic motives—that is, greed—is a powerful one, but a contemporary printer with taste and imagination can make a cheap mass-produced book at least as beautiful as a very costly one made by a printer of mediocre artistic ability. Whenever the printer's art becomes degenerate, lapsing into the excessive use of ornaments, a poor choice of

---

[23] McMurtrie, p. 212.
[24] *Ibid.,* p. 220 *et passim.*
[25] *Ibid.,* pp. 402-404. For an extended study of printing in America, see Margaret Bingham Stillwell's *Incunabula and Americana, 1450-1800: A Key to Bibliographical Study* (2nd ed.; New York: Cooper Square Publishers, 1961, c1930).

typefaces, or the creation of typefaces that call attention to themselves rather than to the writer's thought,[26] then no amount of money can bring about production of good books. Beautiful books can be produced quite economically, if only the persons making them possess those rare qualities of judgment, imagination, and restraint, together with a profound knowledge of the history of their art, essential to sound artistic achievements.[27] While the world may never again see the making of such glorious books as those handwritten wonders of the Middle Ages, which required the full devotion of the energies of thousands of artists inspired (and perhaps driven) by religious hope and fear, there is no economic or technological necessity for making ugly books today. With no extraordinary investment of capital, a printer can create volumes that are esthetically sound and satisfying, even though they can never approach the transcendent beauty of the medieval manuscript book.

The foregoing essay is of course little more than an outline of the vast subject of historical bibliography, and is presented simply to introduce you to the subject and provide a basis for further inquiry into any of its aspects. Note that all of the factual information in the essay has been derived from the work of other writers, all of whom have in turn derived much of their information from the work of others. The primary problem in the writing of this essay—as in the writing of most essays—was a bibliographical one: how to discover what had been written about historical bibliography, how to choose titles most likely to answer the needs of this essay, and finally, how to acquire titles that seemed promising. Once these steps were successfully taken, the task became one of reading, reflecting, taking notes, organizing the notes, and selecting from them materials to be presented in the essay. Until the bibliographical problem was solved, nothing whatever could be done. Sources of factual information must be found before individual facts can be presented, and, for most writers, sources are the published findings of other persons. Those who regard this universally accepted process of scholarship as something not far removed from plagiarism[28] should first judge an analogous case: Is the artist who makes a

---

[26] To no other art is the classical dictum, *Ars est celare artem,* so appropriate as to the art of typography, which can succeed only when the reader is completely unaware of it. For this reason, "arty" or eccentric typefaces have always been failures and always will be.

[27] For an excellent summary of the esthetics of typography, see Stanley Morison's brilliant (and brief) essay, *First Principles of Typography* ("Cambridge Authors' and Printers' Guides," no. 1; Cambridge, England: The University Press, 1951), 17 pp.

[28] Plagiarism is literally theft: the stealing of another person's words or ideas and the representation of them as being one's own. While a conscientious scholar may also make frequent use of other writers' thoughts and phrases, he will normally acknowledge the source of his indebtedness, and add to his sources the distinctive coloring of his own intelligence and personality. The result of scholarship is therefore original, while the result of plagiarism is dishonest repetition.

mosaic portrait or the craftsman who manufactured the colored tiles for him to be credited with the artistry of the portrait?

Every textbook writer is fully conscious of the fact that, when he reaches the end of a chapter, he has left out far more information than he has included. To caution his readers that they have not by any means read the last word on the subject (they have barely read the first), and also to help those who may wish to pursue the subject further on their own, the writer will often list at the end of his chapter "further readings" he thinks worthy of special attention. Unless the subject is exceedingly narrow or special, such lists usually fall far short of the full range of materials published on the subject. The writer may be well aware of their existence, but he cannot devote the space available for his entire book to list all the references to one chapter in it.

Because one of the aims of this book is to teach you how to develop your own list of "further readings" on any subject, such a list is deliberately omitted here. (The titles cited in the footnotes to this chapter might of course be consulted for further information, but they are only a beginning.) As part of your second and third assignments, you will learn *one* of the ways to locate books on a given subject. In the process you are likely to come across a number of books about historical bibliography that will be more appealing to you than those cited in the footnotes of this chapter. Much pleasure comes in knowing how to use a good library properly, in discovering the endless and unexpected subjects and kinds of books you never before knew existed.

# 2

# Descriptive Bibliography

A scholarly book conceived and brought forth by its author with no assistance from other books is almost as rare as a child without ancestors. Few, if any, scholars are capable of writing books so original that nothing in them has been written before. The present generation of scholars sees farther than the previous one not because their vision is better, but because they are standing on the shoulders of their predecessors. Much in the way of fact and argument in any scholarly book will be taken directly from other books, and an honest scholar will let his readers know what those books are, either by identifying them in footnotes to specific passages in his text, or by listing them at the end of his book in an appendix which is commonly called a bibliography, or often by doing both. In both cases the writer is engaged in the practice of descriptive bibliography,[1] which has as its goal the identification of books as physical objects so that a person who has never seen a particular book before can recognize it from the description he has read of it.

The essential fact of descriptive bibliography is its concern with books as physical objects rather than as intellectual products. When you speak simply of James Joyce's novel *Ulysses,* without specifying any of the facts of its publication, you are referring then not to a physical object (a particular book) but to an intellectual entity which may take on a great variety of physical forms. Of this variety, the first edition can be fully described thus:

ULYSSES / by / James Joyce / SHAKESPEARE AND COMPANY / 12, Rue de l'Odeon, 12 / Paris / 1922
   Collation: [xii], 740 pp. [*]², [**]⁴, [1]⁸, 2-46⁸, [47]², 23.7 X 18.5 cm., untrimmed and unopened. Printed on white laid paper.
    Pagination: pp. [i-ii], blank, inserted under folding flaps of outer front cover; pp. [iii-iv], blank; p. [v], fly title; p. [vi], list of books *By the*

---

[1] Or, less precisely, "documentation."

*Same Writer;* p. [vii], title page; p. [viii], copyright notice: ... *Copyright by James Joyce;* p. [ix], limitation notice. *This edition is limited to 1000 copies: / 100 copies (signed) on Dutch / handmade paper numbered from / 1 to 100; 150 copies on vergé / d'Arches numbered from 101 to 250: / 750 copies on handmade paper / numbered from 251 to 1000. /* No. [number stamped in]; p. [x], blank; p. [xi], *The publisher asks the reader's indulgence for typographical errors / unavoidable in the exceptional circumstances. /* S. B.; p. [xii], blank; p. [1], divisional numeral: I; p. [2], blank; pp. [3]-50, text of Part I; p. [51], divisional numeral: II; p. [52], blank; pp. [53]-565, text of Part II; p. [566], blank; p. [567], divisional numeral: III; p. [568], blank; pp. [569]-732, text of Part III; p. [733], colophon: *Printed / for / Sylvia Beach / by / Maurice Darantière at / Dijon, France;* pp. [734-8], blank; pp. [739-40], blank, inserted under folding flaps of outer back cover.

Binding: Blue paper covers. On front cover in white: ULYSSES / BY / JAMES JOYCE.

Publication date and price: February 2, 1922. 150 fr.[2]

With the description and a copy of *Ulysses* in hand, you could determine conclusively whether the book you were holding was a first edition of Joyce's work, even though the description fails to give the slightest clue as to the intellectual or esthetic character of the book. It has only been identified as the physical product of a printing press and a binder's shop, and nothing beyond this is properly a concern of descriptive bibliography. Elaborately detailed descriptions such as this are indispensable for a conclusive, unambiguous identification of a book, but for usual workaday purposes something much briefer and simpler is imperative. It is not unusual for a scholarly book nowadays to contain a bibliography listing several hundred books; if each of them were described as fully as *Ulysses* above, the bibliography might be as long as the book itself. In conventional citation practice, which is all you will be concerned with here, the first edition of Joyce's novel would be described in this highly condensed fashion:

Joyce, James. *Ulysses.* Paris: Shakespeare and Company, 1922.

Here you have the simplest possible form of citation, containing the three most distinctive features of identification: the author's name, the title of his book, and the facts of its publication (that is, *where* it was published, by *whom* it was published, and *when* it was published), always stated in precisely that order in a formal citation. Note that this is the form of citation that you would use in a bibliography (that is, a listing of books given at the end of an essay, chapter, or book, or presented simply as an independent list). The form that you would use as a footnote to identify the

---

[2] This description is taken verbatim from John J. Slocum and Herbert Cahoon, *A Bibliography of James Joyce, 1882-1941* (New Haven: Yale University Press, 1953), pp. 24-25.

source of a particular statement is slightly different. Suppose you had quoted some passage from page 325 of the edition of *Ulysses* cited above. To let your reader know precisely where you had found the passage, so he could verify your transcription of it if he chose to, you would state in a footnote the exact source of the quoted material. In this instance your footnote would read thus:

¹James Joyce, *Ulysses* (Paris: Shakespeare and Company, 1922), p. 325.

By comparing this form with the form given above for a citation of the same book in a bibliography, you will learn the essential differences in form between the two:
1. The footnote always begins with a superscript number corresponding to the numbered passage in the text to which the footnote refers;
2. In the footnote, the author's name is given in uninverted form, Christian name first and family name last, followed by a *comma.* In a bibliography citation, the author's name is inverted, with the Christian name last, followed by a *period;*
3. Footnote and bibliography citations are not punctuated identically. By considering carefully the examples above as well as those that follow, you can discover what the differences are;
4. The footnote usually gives a specific page reference, whereas the bibliography citation refers to the contents of the entire book.

A citation will include all of the following ten elements *that can be found in the book being cited,* and they will always appear in this sequence:

> Author's Name
> Title of the Book
> Editor's Name
> Translator's Name
> Number of Volumes in the Work
> Edition Number
> Series Title
> Place of Publication (usually the name of a city)
> Publisher's Name
> Date of Publication.

By no means will you find all of these items in every book you examine, but you should always search carefully for all of them, because each is a potentially consequential feature of identification and should be omitted only when it cannot be found in the book. Here is a sample citation to an imaginary book that contains all of the listed elements of identification:

Spindleshaft, Elisha Patrick. *On the Anti-Genesis of Anti-Matter.* Ed. George R. Kaulick, tr. Barnaby Barnes. 3 vols. 2nd ed. "Twentieth Century Scientific Series." New York: The Equilibrist's Press, 1965.

Note carefully each detail of punctuation in this bibliography citation, and then consider the points of difference in punctuating the footnote form of the same work:

¹Elisha Patrick Spindleshaft, *On the Anti-Genesis of Anti-Matter,* ed. George R. Kaulick, tr. Barnaby Barnes (3 vols., 2nd ed., "Twentieth Century Scientific Series"; New York: The Equilibrist's Press, 1965), II, 237.

In a footnote citation, the facts of publication (in the above list, everything from "Number of Volumes in the Work" through "Date of Publication") are always placed within parentheses. A footnote citation to a work in more than one volume will normally indicate both the total number of volumes in the entire set and the particular volume number to which reference is being made. In the example above, the first item within the parentheses tells you that the work is in three volumes, and the Roman numeral II preceding the Arabic numeral 237 tells you that reference is being made to page 237 of the second volume in the set. Had reference been made only to the page without specifying the volume, a reader might have to look in all three before finding the passage being cited.

You will usually be able to find all the data you need for making a citation by looking on the title page of the book, on the verso (back side) of the title page, and on the half-title page (the recto of the leaf preceding the title page). In books not published in Great Britain or the United States you will sometimes find some of the facts of publication given on the last page of the book, a survival of the medieval scribal tradition of stating at the end of a handwritten book (which would never have a title page)³ where it was made, who copied it, and when the work was completed. Never make your citation from information on the binding of a book, unless you are unable to find it anywhere else.

As you begin making citations to actual books, you will discover that each of the ten elements above can pose problems to which the solution may not be readily apparent. The following directions will give you some help:

**1. Author's Name.** Transcribe the author's name exactly as you find it on the title page of the book, adding nothing, omitting nothing. Do *not* record titles of honor, or military, ecclesiastical, academic, or other titles, unless they will serve to distinguish between two different authors in your bibliography whose names are identical. Suppose you found this statement

---

³ The first known title page appeared in a book printed in 1463 by Fust and Schöffer, Gutenberg's successors. Gutenberg's famous Bible, printed around the year 1456, had no title page, since he wanted his printed book to resemble in all respects the handwritten books that his customers were accustomed to reading.

on a title page: "By The Reverend Dr. Henry Jones, F. R. S." Your bibliography citation would usually begin thus:

Jones, Henry.

But if your bibliography (that is, your list of works consulted) had another author by the very same name, your citations might begin thus:

Jones, Captain Henry.
Jones, Reverend Dr. Henry, F.R.S.

If there are no more than three authors named on the title page, you will name them all in your citation, in exactly the same order as their names appear on the title page, thus:

Trimble, Timothy; Fusillado, Horatio; and Tickletext, Thomas.

If there are more than three authors named on the title page, you will give only the *first* one named, followed either by the Latin abbreviation *et al.* or the English equivalent "and Others," depending on which language you prefer to speak.

Lewit, Peter, *et al.*

or,

Lewit, Peter, and Others.

The reason for citing the first-named author is that it is under his name that the book will be listed in a library catalog. Should you cite another name, your reader would have difficulty in locating the book in a library.

If the author's name does not appear on the title page or anywhere else in the book, your citation simply begins with the title:

*The History and Theory of Recess in the Primary Schools.*[4]

But if you are able to establish the author's identity from some other source, you may then begin your citation with his name as usual, but placed within square brackets to indicate to your reader that this is information not found in the book itself:

[Fosse, Herakles]. *The History and Theory of Recess in the Primary Schools.*

---

[4] In this example, and others which follow, only as much of the citation is given as is necessary to illustrate the point under discussion.

(Whenever your citation includes *any* information not found in the book itself, it will be put within square brackets as a signal to the reader that you have found it elsewhere. On a library catalog card, however, square brackets are used to indicate that the information was found somewhere other than the title page itself, whether in the book or in some other source.)

When the title page bears only the pseudonym of an author whose real name you know, your citation will begin with the pseudonym, followed by the real name in square brackets:

Twain, Mark [Samuel Langhorne Clemens].

If a pseudonym is identified as such on the title page, but you are unable to supply the real name, you may treat it in this fashion:

Rynne, Xavier (pseud.).

If you spot a pseudonym that is *not* so identified on the title page, but are unable to supply the real name, treat it thus:

Rynne, Xavier [pseud.].

**2. Title.**   Transcribe the title of a book exactly as you find it on the title page, with the following exceptions:

a. It is sometimes necessary to add a punctuation mark to take the place of what amounts to "spatial punctuation" on the title page itself. The following title, in title-page form,

Woman
The Eternal Mystery

would be punctuated like this in a citation:

*Woman: The Eternal Mystery.*

A colon has been added to take the place of the line-spacing on the title page.

b. When a title runs on to undue length, as titles often do in books published prior to the twentieth century, record only as much of the title as is needed to give your reader a clear idea of the nature of the book, and then cut it off, being sure that you have not docked it in the middle of some grammatically complete unit. Add ellipsis marks (three dots) to indicate something has been omitted and terminate the title with a period.

For instance:

> The History and Theory of Recess in the Primary Schools of
> Western Europe
> Together with Some Observations and Animadversions On the
> Deterioration of Recess Theory
> Since the Times of the French Revolution, With Some
> Recommendations for its Rehabilitation And
> Advancement in Our Own Times

would be recorded as follows:

*The History and Theory of Recess in the Primary Schools of Western Europe....*

Parts of the title may also be omitted from the middle but you should *never* omit any of the beginning words of the title, for the simple reason that it is under these words that a title entry for the book will be filed in a library's catalog. Omission of the beginning words of a title is a mistake commonly made, because these words are often in much smaller type on the title page than those that follow.

Underlining the title indicates that the item being cited is a separately published work.[5] The title of an *unpublished* manuscript book would not be underlined; instead, it would appear within quotation marks. The title of a published magazine article would not be underlined, because the article has not been published as a *separate* piece. Its title will appear within quotation marks.

**3. Editor's Name.**   When a book has both a named author and an editor, the editor's name is recorded as follows:

Witwould, Tobias. *A Nonsense Dictionary.* Ed. Aaron Akslegris.

On the title page of the book itself, you might have found the statement, "Edited and with an introduction by Aaron Akslegris," but in your citation this lengthy phrase would be condensed to the essential fact, "Ed. Aaron Akslegris."

Now suppose, as often happens with dictionaries and other composite writings, just the editor, no author, is named on the title page. Your citation would then read:

Beorship, Toby (ed.). *A Dictionary of Tiddleywinks.*

---

[5] Underlining in manuscript or typescript is the equivalent of using italics in typography. Where italics are used in this book, you would underline instead, unless you happened to be setting type.

If the editor is called a compiler rather than an editor on the title page, then use the abbreviation "comp." with his name instead of "ed."

Treat editors' names in all other respects exactly as you do authors', omitting titles of honor, citing no more than three names, and so on.

**4. Translator's Name.** Translators' names appear thus:

Backov, Boris. *A Lullaby for Lenin.* Tr. Thomas R. Hacque.

[Note: illustrators are not ordinarily identified, unless it is because of their work that you consulted the book in the first place. If, for example, you made a study of Phiz's illustrations of Dickens's novels and cited one of the novels in which his drawings appeared, your citation would naturally indicate that the edition you had used was illustrated by Phiz.]

**5. Number of Volumes.** When a work is in only one volume, you make no statement of this fact. But if it is in more than one volume, then you indicate the number of volumes in the entire set.

Pfnner, Stanley. *Piscatory Paradise.* 4 vols.

Be careful that you are not fooled into thinking that because you see four volumes of a book on the shelf, the book contains only four volumes. What if someone has checked out volumes five through twenty-five? Or suppose the work is still in progress, and only the first four volumes have been published so far? Unless you can determine with certainty that the work contains no more volumes than you can find on the shelf, then your citation should read like this:

Pfnner, Stanley. *Piscatory Paradise.* Vols. 1-4.

Sometimes a single volume in a set will have its own distinctive subtitle, and then, if you wish, you may cite that single volume instead of the entire set.

Appalachia's White Hope
Higher Education in Western Carolina
(In Four Volumes)
by
Dr. Algernon Addlepate and Prof. Talmadge Turnpage, M. A.
Volume Two
The Frenzied Years

Here your citation may take one of two possible forms:

Addlepate, Algernon, and Turnpage, Talmadge. *Appalachia's White Hope: Higher Education in Western Carolina,* Vol. II: *The Frenzied Years.*

Or,

Addlepate, Algernon, and Turnpage, Talmadge. *Appalachia's White Hope: Higher Education in Western Carolina.* 4 vols.

Note that in the first form no statement is made respecting number of volumes, since volume two is only one volume.

**6. Edition Number.** When a book is published in a substantially revised form it may be given a distinctive edition number by the publisher. When an edition number is given in the book itself, it should always be recorded in your citation, because this is a significant feature of the book's identification. If you quote a passage from the third edition of a book and fail to specify the edition in your citation, your reader may very well search for the passage in the first edition and fail to find it. It is your duty to spare your readers this kind of exasperation; they may be having difficulty enough just in reading your paper.

When no edition number is given in the book, your citation will pass over this fact in silence. Do not confuse "printings" and "impressions" with editions. The third edition of a book, for example, will differ substantially from all other editions of that book; the text has been altered, and type has been reset for printing the new edition. But often a book will be reprinted many times from the original plates, with no significant changes being made in the text, and then you may find (usually on the verso of the title page) some such statement as "Fifth printing," or "Fifth impression" (both mean the same thing), which publishers put there to let you know how popular the book has been. But since the fifth printing of any given edition of a book is virtually identical with any other printing of the same edition, the number of the printing is not usually recorded in a citation. If in your citations you should confuse printings or impressions with editions, you will lead your readers far astray. The fourth edition of the following book should be cited as follows:

Pfnner, Stanley. *Piscatory Paradise.* 4 vols. 4th ed.

But if you found in an earlier edition of this book a statement or statements to the effect that this was the fourth *printing* of the first *edition,* then your citation would begin:

Pfnner, Stanley. *Piscatory Paradise.* 4 vols. 1st ed.

The edition number is always recorded, but the printing number is omitted.

**7. Series Title.** The series title is recorded in its entirety and placed within quotation marks.

Pfnner, Stanley. *Piscatory Paradise.* Ed. Merlin Giles, tr. Quentin Durward. 4 vols.
2nd ed. "The Compleat Angler's Library."

The names of editors of a series are not recorded. The chief problem with the series title is to recognize one when you see it. When a number of books by different authors, but similar in format, scope, or subject, and, usually, issued by the same publisher, are given a common title in addition to their individual titles, that common title is known as a series title, and often it can give you some useful implications about the type and quality of all the books in that series. In any case you should be able to distinguish a series title from an ordinary book title, or you are liable to confuse the two and make ludicrous mistakes in your citation. Series titles are often found on the half-title page, but they sometimes appear on the title page itself or on its verso. The words *Library, Publications, Lectures, Series, Studies, Memoirs, Monographs,* and *Contributions* will often appear in a series title; whenever you see them, you should consider carefully the possibility that you have before you a series rather than an individual book title. Examples:

> Modern Library of the World's Best Books.
> Religion and Civilization Series.
> Publications of the Prince Society, Boston.
> Studies in Biblical Theology.
> Monographs on Physiology.
> Contributions to Economic Analysis.

**8. Place of Publication.** If more than one place of publication is given in the book, cite the place that is named first (the name of a town, not a state or nation), unless some other place is more prominently displayed on the title page, through use of larger type, central position, etc. Do not in any case cite more than one place. If no place is named, use the abbreviation N.p.

Pfnner, Stanley. *Piscatory Paradise.* Ed. Merlin Giles, tr. Quentin Durward. 4 vols.
2nd ed. "The Compleat Angler's Library." N.p.:

**9. Publisher's Name.** If more than one publisher is named, cite the one that is named first, unless some other publisher's name is more prominently displayed. If no publisher is named, pass over this fact in silence. If both a publisher and a printer are named cite the publisher; if a printer is named but the publisher is not, cite the printer. (The publisher is the man who undertakes the responsibility of getting the book printed and sold; the printer merely prints it and has nothing further to do with it.)

Pfnner, Stanley. *Piscatory Paradise.* Ed. Merlin Giles, tr. Quentin Durward. 4 vols.
    3rd ed. "The Compleat Angler's Library." New York: Bookmaster Press.

**10. Date of Publication.** Give the most recent date you can find in the
book. If you also find an earlier date in the book preceded by the letter c
(c1921), this is the copyright date, whereas the most recent date is the date
of printing. The copyright date often gives a more reliable indication of
when the book was actually written, and if you think it worthwhile to let
your reader know that a book was copyrighted a long time before its most
recent printing, then give both the printing and the copyright dates.

Pfnner, Stanley. *Piscatory Paradise.* Ed. Merlin Giles, tr. Quentin Durward. 4 vols.
    3rd ed. "The Compleat Angler's Library." New York: Bookmaster Press,
    1960, c 1921.

You will find the solution to many other special problems of citation
practice in chapter five of Kate L. Turabian's *Student's Guide for Writing
College Papers* ("Phoenix Books"; Chicago: The University of Chicago
Press, 1964), which you may wish to refer to whenever you run into
seemingly insoluble predicaments.

    The story is told of an old sea captain who, each morning before he did
anything else, would unlock his desk drawer, gaze briefly in it, lock it up,
then go about his day's work. When he died, his quartermaster, who had
observed this ritual for years with intense and unsatisfied curiosity,
immediately unlocked the captain's desk and stared in the drawer. What he
saw was a single piece of paper, with the statement written on it in a bold
hand, "Port is left, starboard is right."

    You can avoid the captain's perplexity by *memorizing* at the outset the
list of ten elements that may appear in a standard book citation, and
learning the punctuation patterns for both the bibliography and the
footnote forms. With that much of the problem under control, you will find
the multifarious details and special cases much easier to handle, since you
have a basic framework on which to hang them.

    So much for the bibliographical description of whole books. There is a
still more numerous class of writings that you must be able to describe:
articles in periodicals, and individual essays or other writings included in a
collection published in book form. The essential features of identification
are the same as those for a book (author, title, and facts of publication), but
the description of the facts of publication is usually somewhat more
elaborate because the facts themselves are often more elaborate.

    There are two slightly different forms of citation for periodical articles.
One is for the *scholarly* periodical, the kind of publication in which scholars
publish the results of their most recent research; the other is for *popular*
periodicals, titles such as *Life, Time, The New Yorker,* and *Playboy,* which

are addressed to an audience of general readers and are concerned with topics of general, rather than special, interest.

A citation for a *scholarly* periodical article normally specifies the following facts in the order given:

> Author's Name
> Title of the Article (in quotation marks)
> Title of the Periodical (underlined)
> Volume Number of the Periodical
> Issue Number of the Periodical
> Date of Publication (in parentheses)
> Inclusive Paging of the Article.

Here is a typical bibliography citation exhibiting all of these features:

Roebuck, Carl. "The Economic Development of Ionia," *Classical Philology,* XLVIII, No. 3 (January, 1953), 9-16.

What this citation tells a reader is that in the third issue of volume forty-eight of a periodical entitled *Classical Philology,* which was published in January, 1953, he will find between pages nine and sixteen an article by Carl Roebuck entitled "The Economic Development of Ionia." Note especially that the editor of a periodical is *never* named in citing an article in it, nor is the place of publication or the publisher's name given, even though this information can usually be found in the periodical itself. These things are omitted because they are not essential to the identification of a periodical, although they are in the case of books.

It is common practice to give the volume number of a periodical in the area of humanities in Roman numerals (even if it is in Arabic numerals on the periodical itself), whereas scientists prefer to give volume numbers of their periodicals in Arabic numerals. The latter practice is certainly the saner, while the other is simply traditional. In writing a term paper, the only safe course to follow is the one set by your instructor. If writing for publication, you will have to follow the style of the journal in which your paper is to be published.

As with books, a slightly different form is required for a footnote citation of a periodical article:

¹ Carl Roebuck, "The Economic Development of Ionia," *Classical Philology,* XLVIII, No. 3 (January, 1953), 13.

(The assumption here is that the footnote is intended to refer the reader to some passage on page thirteen of Mr. Roebuck's article.)

There are three differences between forms for bibliography and footnote citations of a periodical article:

1. The footnote citation begins with the superscript number, which is keyed to the passage in the text to which the footnote refers;

2. As with books, the author's name in a footnote citation is given in uninverted form, followed by a comma instead of a period; and

3. In the footnote form, a specific page reference is usually given, instead of the inclusive paging of the entire article.

Now for citations of *popular* periodical articles. They differ from the scholarly only in being a little simpler: volume and issue numbers are omitted, and the date of publication is not put within parentheses.

Turner, E. S. "The Rules of Infamous Conduct," *Punch,* April 20, 1966, pp. 573-74.

¹ E. S. Turner, "The Rules of Infamous Conduct," *Punch,* April 20, 1966, p. 574.

The same form is used for newspaper articles:

"A Hero on Sunday, Seized in Brooklyn as Thief on Monday," *New York Times,* May 31, 1966, p. 35.

(The footnote form follows the pattern of that immediately above.)

The most complex form we will discuss here is one that is required in citing an essay (or poem, short story, etc.) by one writer that appears as part of a collection edited by another writer. Again the problem is simply to identify the author of the essay, the title of the essay, and the facts of its publication, the last of which requires the complete identification of the book in which the essay appears. A sample citation will make this situation a little more easily comprehensible:

Bradley, A. C. "Shakespearean Tragedy," in *Readings on the Character of Hamlet, 1616-1947,* ed. Claude C. H. Williamson. London: Allen & Unwin, 1950, pp. 289-97.

The import of this citation is that in a collection of essays edited by Claude Williamson and entitled *Readings on the Character of Hamlet, 1616-1947,* published in London by Allen & Unwin in 1950, you will find, between pages 289 and 297, an essay by A. C. Bradley with the title "Shakespearean Tragedy." Note the meaning of the italics and quotation marks in this citation. A footnote citation to, say, page 294 of this essay would read as follows:

¹ A. C. Bradley, "Shakespearean Tragedy," in *Readings on the Character of Hamlet, 1616-1947,* ed. Claude C. H. Williamson (London: Allen & Unwin, 1950), p. 294.

However complex the form you may encounter, you will always be able to reach an adequate solution to the problem of citation if you keep in mind the essential elements of bibliographical description listed above for books and periodical articles, and the sequence in which they should be written. Also, remember that Turabian's *Student's Guide* gives a wide range of sample citations, among which you will usually be able to find one whose pattern will be precisely applicable to some specific problem of citation that may perplex you.

A bibliography such as you might append to a term paper or thesis may list many items of diverse form: books, periodical articles, unpublished manuscripts, government documents, records of interviews, and so on. When this is the case, it is customary to group your material by form, and then sub-arrange the items in each group alphabetically by author, or, if no author is named, by title. Thus your bibliography might list first all the government documents you had consulted, then the periodical articles, then the books, then the manuscripts, and finally the interviews. But in a bibliography of very slight extent—no more than ten or fifteen items—there would be little reason for a classified arrangement, and you would then list all your entries in one sequence, alphabetically by author or editor, depending upon the form of the citation, or by title if the work has no identifiable author or editor.

When you list in succession two or more items by the same author, your second and all subsequent citations may omit the author's name and begin instead with a long dash (ten spaces will do, but practice varies):

Pokethankertscheff, Vladinmire R. *How to Advance Progressively Backwards.* New York, 1929.

_____. *Out of the Morass and into the Mire.* Boston: The Serendipity Press, 1939.

## KNOWING WHEN TO USE A FOOTNOTE CITATION

As a general rule, it is proper, and often necessary, to indicate in a footnote citation the source of any direct quotation in the text of your paper, any assertion of fact derived from the work of another person, or even a paraphrased idea that you have taken from someone else. If followed scrupulously, this rule would lead to the writing of papers so pestered and becluttered with footnotes that your readers would be hampered rather than helped by your zealousness. So exceptions to the rule are necessary. But as a beginning scholar you will do well to err in making too many footnotes than in making too few. As your judgment matures, and you have wider experience with the footnoting habits of competent professional scholars, you will become more adept at the art of omitting unnecessary footnotes. One *general* exception to the general rule of citing sources is this: when stating a fact that is commonly known and is not a matter of controversy, you need not cite the source, since no one is likely to be interested in it. For example, statements of fact such as the following would not require citations:

> Because the earth is round, not flat. . . .or, When Shakespeare died in 1616. . . .or, The invention of the art of printing from movable types was one of the triumphant achievements of the Renaissance.

You may even omit citations to direct quotations when the passage is one that most readers would be expected to recognize. It would insult your reader's intelligence to tell him where he should go to find the line "To be, or not to be: that is the question."

You have perhaps noticed that many textbook writers give no footnote citations whatever. This is not a pretense on their part that the statements they have made are original with them, but rather an admission that virtually everything they say about their subject is now very generally assented to by other scholars and is no longer actively debated. The aim of a textbook writer is not to produce new knowledge, but to consolidate what has already been established by others. But whenever a textbook touches on a subject that is still being disputed, you may then expect the writer to cite one or more of the publications in which the debate is being conducted.

## SECOND AND SUBSEQUENT FOOTNOTE REFERENCES TO THE SAME WORK

Your first footnote citation of a particular book, periodical article, etc., will always be in the full form as shown in the examples above. But having cited a work once in your paper, you will often make repeated footnote references to it, and it is then possible to make your citation in a greatly condensed form. There are two systems currently used for this purpose, but we will consider here only the simpler one.

Suppose your first footnote citation of Pfnner's book is as follows:

¹ Stanley Pfnner, *Piscatory Paradise,* ed. Merlin Giles, tr. Quentin Durward (4 vols. 3rd ed., "The Compleat Angler's Library"; New York: Bookmaster Press, 1960, c1921), II, 235.

Now suppose that your second footnote is a citation of the same work: how can you avoid the tedious business of copying this lengthy citation again? Simply make your second citation as follows:

² *Ibid.,* III, 127.

The Latin abbreviation *Ibid.* means (in a footnote) "This is the same work I just cited," so it is necessary to give only the specific volume and page number of the work to let your reader know exactly to what passage reference has been made.

Now suppose that your third footnote cites an entirely different work:

³ Arnold Tacklebachs, *Big Two-Hearted Creek* (N.p.: Trident Publishers, n.d.), p. 65.

Your fourth footnote citation reads:

⁴ *Ibid.,* p. 286.

To which book does this *Ibid.* refer? To the one immediately preceding: Tacklebachs's.

Now in your fifth footnote you wish to refer once more to Pfnner's book. *Ibid.* won't work, because it will refer now to Tacklebachs's book. The solution to your problem is this:

⁵ Pfnner, II, 236.

Since you have cited thus far only one book by Pfnner, this shorthand reference is completely unambiguous and will serve. But suppose now that your sixth footnote is this:

⁶ Stanley Pfnner, *Angling for Moby Dick* (New Bedford: The Ishmael Press, 1948), p. 37.

In your seventh footnote, you wish to cite this same book again and may do so as follows:

⁷ *Ibid.,* p. 93.

But if in your eighth footnote you wish to cite Pfnner's *Piscatory Paradise* once more, you can use neither *Ibid.* nor simply the author's last name (as you did in footnote 5), since you have now cited two works by the same author, and his name by itself would be ambiguous. Here is your way out:

⁸ Pfnner, *Piscatory Paradise,* IV, 187.

If you are properly considerate of your reader, you will use none of the shorthand devices (except possibly the last) when they refer the reader to earlier footnotes that are many pages away. If footnote 7 (above) fell twenty pages farther along in your paper than footnote 6, it would be rather bothersome to your reader to try to find out just what your *Ibid.* meant. But if only a page or two intervened, then the *Ibid.* would cause no hardship. The purpose of formal citation practice is to make life a little easier for your reader: any device that thwarts that purpose should be abandoned.

While there is little intellectual stimulation to be found in descriptive bibliography on the primitive level of conventional citation practice which you are concerned with here, mastery of the basic forms at the outset of your academic career will spare you (and your readers) some confusion later on. Almost every paper that you write as a college student will require you to make competent citations to the materials that you have drawn upon because it is a point of intellectual honesty (in most cases) to reveal to your reader not only the exact sources of quoted materials, but also the sources of ideas, arguments, and points of view that you may have paraphrased from the writings of other persons. Books are the scholar's tools: a scholar who cannot describe them correctly cuts as absurd a figure as a carpenter who cannot tell a hammer from a handsaw, and draws suspicion on the merit of all his work when he fails to identify, or fails to identify correctly, the books that have contributed to his own composition.

Now that you know how to describe books, we will go on, in the succeeding chapters, to some of the problems of locating books, which of course you must be able to do in order to describe them.

# 3

# The Subject Catalog

"Woe be to him that reads but one book."[1] A proper understanding of any subject demands the reading of several, perhaps many, books, but often at the beginning of a study the writer knows neither the titles nor authors of any books on the subject he is investigating. The shortest way out of this predicament is to consult the library's subject catalog,[2] which is a record of the books the library owns arranged alphabetically in the order of their subjects. If you are interested in mythology but do not yet know Bulfinch's famous book, or Sir James Frazer's *magnum opus,* or anything else in the extensive literature of this subject, you could quickly discover these books and others like them by going to the subject catalog and looking for the term "Mythology" typed as a heading on the catalog cards.

Now this procedure seems simple enough on its surface, but in practice certain complications arise that will seriously impair your use of the subject catalog until you have learned how to deal with them. First there is the formidable problem of terminology. To get a meaningful response from the subject catalog, you must speak to it in its own language, the vocabulary of which is often completely unpredictable. Suppose you wanted to find a

[1] The source of a quotation used simply for the sake of embellishment, not as a point of argument or assertion of fact, is usually not identified. A formal citation for the quotation above would be as unnecessary as it was pretentious.

[2] The card catalogs of some libraries are divided into two sections, one of which contains only subject entries, while the other contains author and title entries. Such a catalog is called a "divided catalog"; the section of it which contains subject entries is called the "subject catalog," while the other section is called the "author-title catalog." Whenever you want a book *about* a particular subject, whether the subject be a person, place, thing, or idea, you must, therefore, consult the subject catalog. But in other libraries, subject entries are interfiled with all other kinds of entries, so there is only one catalog instead of two. This is called a "dictionary catalog." Whenever the term "subject catalog" is used in this book, as a matter of convenience it will be understood to mean either the subject section of a divided catalog (as it normally does) or the entire system of subject entries in a dictionary catalog. Go take a look at the catalog of your library right now and determine whether it is a dictionary or a divided catalog.

history of France, and went to the subject catalog for help. You would first
have to determine what terminology the catalog employs for that subject.
Would it be "French history," or "History of France," or "History of the
French people," or "History—France," or perhaps "France—History"?
Reflection and logical deduction are useless here, since one form is just as
appropriate as another. The form that is actually used is "France
—History," and now that you know this form you should remember
it, since the pattern is repeated for all histories of all other nations
and subjects as well.

The linguistic form that is chosen to designate a particular subject in
the catalog is known as a subject heading. "France—History" is therefore a
subject heading, but "French History," "History of France," "History of
the French people," and "History—France" are *not* subject headings. To
obtain a meaningful response from the subject catalog, you must approach
it with the exact language of its subject headings. Thus if you sought a
work on French history under the form "French history" you would get no
response from the catalog because that form is not a subject heading and
nothing would ever be entered under it. Unless you know the correct
subject-heading form when you consult the catalog, you cannot be sure, in
the event of a negative result, whether the reason for your failure to find an
entry was that the library had no books on the subject, or that you were
looking for them under the wrong subject-heading form.

How then do you determine the correct subject-heading forms of the
infinite variety of subjects about which the library may own books? First,
you should know by heart a few of the basic forms for history, language,
literature, art, music, and philosophy, for you will often search the subject
catalog for materials in these fields. The form for history you already know:
the name of the nation or the subject with the subdivision "History." The
form for language is the name of the language *plus* the word "language": a
book about the French language would be entered not under "French," but
under "French language." You might expect the form for literature to be
patterned after that for history, with the term "Literature" used as
subdivision of the name of a nation, but it is not. For reasons too intricate
to explain here, the system of subject headings lacks the perfect consistency
that you might expect of it, but you can learn to cope with this deficiency by
using your imagination and keeping alert to the various possibilities of form
in the construction of subject headings. The subject-heading form for
French literature is just that: "French literature," rather than
"France—literature," which the form for history might induce you to
expect. Specific forms of literature have specific subject-heading forms:
"French drama," "French fiction," "French poetry," "French essays." If
you wanted to find a book about the French novel, you would, therefore,
look under "French fiction" rather than "French literature," this being the
more specifically applicable of the two headings. Subject headings for the
art, music, and philosophy of a nation take this form: "Art, French,"

"Music, French," "Philosophy, French," rather than the form "French art," etc., which you might expect from the form for literature.

Here are six basic headings that you should *memorize* because they will serve as patterns in areas that are likely to be of continuing interest to you:

> France—History
> French language
> French literature
> Art, French
> Music, French
> Philosophy, French

Since it is sometimes impossible to specify a single subject with a single word, as you have already learned from the examples above, a variety of linguistic forms is used in the construction of subject headings. Familiarity with the several patterns that are used will give you some help with the terminological problem of subject headings.

**Proper Nouns.**   Names of persons, places, buildings, ships, societies, institutions, government agencies, etc., may be used as subject headings. If you wanted a book *about* Shakespeare, you would look in the subject catalog under the heading "Shakespeare, William." But if you wanted a book that Shakespeare wrote, you would then look in the author-title catalog. A book about the city of Asheville would be entered under the heading "Asheville, N. C."

**The Single Noun Form.**   The simplest linguistic form a subject heading may take is the single noun, unmodified and without a qualifying phrase to explain or limit it. Examples of such headings are "Botany," "Mathematics," "Despotism," "Emotions," and "Manuscripts."

**The Uninverted Adjectival Phrase.**   This form consists of an adjective followed by the noun modified, as in the headings "Agricultural credit," "Real property," "Pythagorean proposition," "English literature," and "Indian warfare."

**The Inverted Adjectival Phrase.**   This form contains the same elements as the one above, but the noun precedes the adjective that modifies it: thus we find "Art, French" (instead of "French art"), "Geography, Economic" (instead of "Economic geography"), and so on. Whenever an inverted form is used in the subject catalog, a cross reference will be made to it from the uninverted form. In the case of "Art, French," you will find a cross reference reading "French art *see* Art, French."

**Phrase Headings with Two Nouns.**   These headings consist of two nouns with or without modifiers, connected by a preposition or conjunction: "Slavery in the U. S.," "Germans in South Africa," "Women as authors," "Electricity on ships," "Photography of children," "Divine right of kings," "Figures of speech," "Literature and morals," "Overland journeys to the Pacific," "Church and education," "Religion and science," "Art and science." Cross references are usually made to these forms from a form beginning with the last term in the phrase: "Kings, Divine right of *see* Divine right of kings"; or "Science and art *see* Art and science."

**Inverted Phrase Headings with Two or More Nouns.**    These headings are similar to those just discussed, except that the noun which would grammatically come last is placed at the beginning of the phrase: "Debt, Imprisonment for"; "Plants, Protection of"; "Plans, Effect of Prayer on." Cross references will be made from the uninverted form: "Imprisonment for debt *see* Debt, Imprisonment for."

**Subdivided Forms.**    All of the forms discussed above can have subdivisions, which may generally be described as form, topical, geographical, or chronological. In the subject catalog the subdivisions of a heading will always be typed after a long dash following the main heading: "France—History."

The range of form subdivisions is so large that it would be pointless to enumerate them all, but there are a few that are so widely used that you might profitably become acquainted with them:

> Bibliography
> Bio-Bibliography
> Collections
> Dictionaries and encyclopedias
> Handbooks, manuals, etc.
> History
> Indexes
> Outlines, syllabi, etc.
> Periodicals
> Yearbooks

Most subjects are capable of geographical subdivision, as, for example, "Birds—Canada," "Birds—France," "Birds—U.S.," and so on. Moreover, when a place name is used as a main heading, it is always capable of form and topical subdivision: "U.S.—Bibliography," "U.S.—Biography," "U.S.—Civilization," "U.S.—History," and so on. This raises an interesting problem: how do you know, when you consult the subject catalog for a book on birds of the U.S., whether to look for "Birds—U.S." or "U.S.—Birds"? Not only do you not know which term will come first, there is no way for you to deduce logically what the sequence will be. But if you will follow this simple rule, the catalog should always settle the problem for you: whenever you are interested in a topic that has some geographical aspect, always look first for the name of the region with the topic as a subdivision. Then if the library actually owns a book on the subject, you will find either the subject heading you are seeking or a cross reference to it.[3] In the example above, had you looked in the subject catalog under "U.S.—Birds" you should have found a cross reference saying "*See* Birds—U.S.," and of course under this latter form you would find entries for the books you needed.

Many subjects have some chronological aspect, and this is indicated in the subject heading by a subdivision which specifies the time period to which the particular heading is limited, as, for example, "U.S.—Civilization—20th century." Consider the following list of headings, which appear in their exact catalog sequence:

> U.S.—Civilization
> U.S.—Civilization—Addresses, essays, lectures
> U.S.—Civilization—Anecdotes, facetiae, satires
> U.S.—Civilization—German influences
> U.S.—Civilization—History
> U.S.—Civilization—Periodicals
> U.S.—Civilization—1783-1865
> U.S.—Civilization—20th century
> U.S.—Civilization—1918-1945

Notice that the chronological subdivisions have been filed after all other kinds of subdivision, and that they are arranged in chronological rather than alphabetical order. To interfile them with other subdivisions in alphabetical order would make them very difficult to find, especially if the cataloger had chosen some name for a period which you did not know, and it would also put them in chaotic order with respect to each other (try arranging the numbers one through ten in alphabetical order and see what happens). Of course, if you forget the principle of filing chronological subdivisions, you will have difficulty finding them too; but that will be your own fault, not the cataloger's. Chronological subdivisions are not, as the example above might imply, limited to geographical headings. Consider the following list of headings:

> American literature—History and criticism
> American literature—Massachusetts
> American literature—New England
> American literature—North Carolina
> American literature—Outlines, syllabi, etc.

---

[3] That is, you *ought* to find a cross reference, but in many libraries you will not, because the cataloger failed to put it there, not realizing how useful it would be to you. Now go look in your catalog for the subject entry "U. S.—Birds," and if you do not find a cross reference from that form, go see your library director and recommend to him that such cross references be installed in his catalog, because they would be most helpful to his patrons. It is very difficult for him to know what you need unless you tell him; if your library serves you poorly, it is partly your own fault for not speaking up.

American literature — Study and teaching
American literature — Virginia
American literature — Colonial period
American literature — Revolutionary period
American literature — Early 18th century
American literature — 19th century
American literature — Early 19th century
American literature — 20th century
American literature — 20th century — Bibliography
American literature — 20th century — History and criticism

In this list the chronological sequence begins with the subdivision "Colonial period" and proceeds in strict chronological order from the earliest period to the most recent. Note that chronological subdivisions can be further subdivided by form or topic, as in the last three headings in the list.

Until you have become better acquainted with the form and sequence of subdivisions in the subject catalog, you would do well to examine all the subdivisions under any main heading that you come upon in an actual search problem. Otherwise you may fail to discover the subdivision that is most specifically applicable to the subject in question.

One final comment about subject-heading forms: Often you will want to find a book about another book. For example, you may wish to find a book about Shakespeare's play *Hamlet*. To find it, you will have to look in the subject catalog, first, under the author's name and, then, under the subdivision "Hamlet," thus: "Shakespeare, William — Hamlet." If you should look instead directly under the title "Hamlet" in the subject catalog (filed with other headings beginning H_____), you would find nothing and might wrongly conclude that your library owned no books about that play. If, however, you want a copy of the play itself, you will find it in the author-title catalog, either under the author entry "Shakespeare, William," or under the title entry "Hamlet."

As a matter of general procedure in using the subject catalog, you should *always* look first for a subject heading that corresponds to the *specific* subject in which you are interested. If you want a book on canaries, look first for the specific heading "Canaries," not for the more general heading "Birds" or "Zoology." If you fail to find any entries under the specific heading (and you have ascertained that such a subject heading actually exists), then you might well look for a book under a more general heading, because it might have some information on your subject, though it probably would not give an extended treatment of it. Thus if you found nothing under the heading "Canaries" in the subject catalog, you might then consider the books listed under the more general heading "Birds," since many of them may contain some material on canaries, however slight. If you want a book on French painting, you would begin your search with the most specific heading, "Painting, French," and then move to more general ones as the occasion demanded, such as "Art, French," or simply "Painting" or "Art." If you want a book about a particular French artist, say Claude Monet, look first under the specific heading "Monet, Claude," and if need be consult the more general headings "Painters, French," "Painting, French," "Artists, French," and "Art, French." If you want a history of Brazil, first try "Brazil—History," and if you find nothing there or want additional material then use the more general heading "South America—History." To make the subject catalog fully productive, you must bring a certain amount of reflection and imagination to the process, as well as a general understanding of procedural techniques.

After seeing some of the elaborately subdivided headings such as "American literature—20th century—History and criticism," students begin to suspect that most subject headings will take on the most complex form possible. Readers who want a biography of George Washington are prone to invent such elaborate headings as "Biography—U. S.—Presidents—George Washington," when in fact the heading is simply (and specifically) "Washington, George." A study of Keats' poetry is likely to be sought under "English literature—Poets—John Keats," when the heading is simply "Keats, John." The only reason for the existence of such intricate headings as "American literature—20th century—History and criticism" is the virtual impossibility of stating the subject in any simpler manner. With rare exceptions, subject headings are stated in the most specific terms possible. It is therefore good practice to search first for the most specific description of a subject you can imagine.

The arrangement of subject headings in the catalog is alphabetical, not logical, and this is both a virtue and a defect. The sequence Arson, Art, Arteries, is wholly illogical, for the three things have absolutely nothing in common, but the order is alphabetically correct, making the terms easy to find in any extensive list. On the other hand, the sequence Biology, Zoology, Vertebrates, Canines, Dachshunds, is a logical order of terms moving directly from the most general to the most specific, but alphabetically it is chaos. Now it is possible to arrange the headings in a subject catalog logically, and this would have the great merit of bringing together in one sequence all the elements of a given subject, but it would make the finding of a specific heading exceedingly difficult. In a logically not alphabetically) arranged catalog, if you wanted a book about dachshunds, you would have to look first under the heading "Biology" and then proceed through the series of subdivisions "Zoology," "Vertebrates," and "Canines" until at last you reached the final division "Dachshunds"—a dogged search indeed. In an alphabetically arranged catalog, you would proceed directly to the term "Dachshunds," but all the related headings about other species of dogs would be scattered throughout the catalog.

Since the alphabetically arranged subject catalog is defective logically, a system of cross references (known as "see-also references") has been developed to indicate under a given heading any other headings that are related to it. In some libraries you will find these see-also references filed in the catalog itself, but they are not always reliable. We will assume that your catalog does not have them; but they are still available in a huge book entitled *Subject Headings Used in the Dictionary Catalogs of the Library of Congress,* one or more copies of which should be placed somewhere convenient to your catalog. (If there are none, then ask your librarian to have one placed there.) Excluding proper nouns, this book lists all the subject headings that you will find in your catalog, and many that you will not find, since your library will not own books on as many subjects as the Library of Congress does. Under many of the headings in this list you will find a list of related headings. Here is the entry for "Frontier and pioneer life" in the Library of Congress list (ignore the terms listed after the x and xx which follow those listed below):

> Frontier and pioneer life.
>> *sa* Cowboys
>> Indians of North America—Captivities
>> Land claim associations
>> Overland journeys to the Pacific
>> Pioneers
>> Ranch life
>> Wild men

The abbreviation "sa" stands for "see also," and the intent of the list is to suggest that you see also the several headings that are related to the subject of frontier and pioneer life. These lists of see-also references can often help you pinpoint the subject heading that is most specifically applicable to your topic. They can also be useful in helping you determine the precise linguistic form a subject heading may take. If you wanted to find a book about cross-country journeys in the days of the American frontier, no amount of independent speculation would ever lead you to conclude that the appropriate subject-heading form was "Overland journeys to the Pacific." But you might readily deduce that such journeys had something to do with frontier life, and by turning to the heading for that subject and reading quickly down the list of see-also references, you would come upon the heading "Overland journeys to the Pacific," which you would recognize as the appropriate one for your quest, even though it would never have occurred to you that the heading might take that form.

Note carefully the difference between a "see" reference and a "see-also" reference. The see reference leads you from a non-subject-heading form to a subject heading, while a see-also reference leads you from one subject heading to other subject headings related to it. For example, the cross reference "French art, *see* Art, French," is a see reference, leading you from a non-subject heading (French art) to a subject heading (Art, French).

Most library catalogs will have all the necessary see references in the catalog itself. But many catalogs will not contain all the see-also references, so you will have to consult the Library of Congress subject-heading list to find them.

Of course, your library may not own books on all the subjects which the Library of Congress list invites you to see also, so you may find no entries in your catalog under some of the references. If you think your library ought to buy some books on those missing subjects, by all means let your librarian know so he can get them for you.

The chief problem in using the subject catalog, as you have seen, is to determine precisely what subject-heading form has been employed to designate a particular topic. Intelligent use of the subject-heading list is the best solution to that problem. Before approaching the subject catalog itself, you should always ascertain from the subject-heading list the exact form you need, and *then* go to the catalog and see if the library actually owns any books on that subject. This is not so simple a process as going directly to the subject catalog and trying to imagine what form a particular subject heading will take, but it is a far more reliable one. There is no other way to be sure of getting maximum yield from the subject catalog. The process is actually not so complicated as it may sound; and the various exercises relating to this assignment will bring into focus much that may now seem confusing.

Subject headings that have been assigned to any particular book are usually listed at the bottom of the catalog card:

---

PE          Wise, Claude Merton, 1887–
1135            Applied phonetics. Illustrated by H. S. Wise.
W5.7        Englewood Cliffs, N.J., Prentice-Hall, 1957.
               546 p. illus. 24 cm.


               Includes bibliographies.


               1. English language—Phonetics. 2. English
            language—Pronunciation. 3. English
            language—Dialects—U.S.     I. Title

---

The subject headings are those items which follow the Arabic (*not* the Roman) numerals in the lower paragraph. Often you can get a much better idea of what a book is about by looking at these subject headings than you can from the title of the book itself. The title *Applied Phonetics* in the example above does not even tell you whether one or many languages are being considered, nor does it indicate any concern with American dialects; but the subject headings tell you this quite plainly.

When there are two or more subject headings listed at the bottom of the catalog card, they can serve you very nicely as see-also references to each other. Suppose you found the card above in the subject catalog with the heading "English language—Phonetics" typed at the top of it. By looking at the complete list of headings in the last paragraph of the card, you would, in effect, be invited to see also the entries filed under "English language—Pronunciation" and "English language—Dialects," as these subjects are presumably related, having been treated together within the covers of one book. Then you could check the cards under *those* headings, and add to your list any new subject headings which you found in the last paragraph of those cards. As you see, this process can be extended until you have a very complete chain of related subject headings, from which you may select those which are most appropriate to your interests. The process is actually much simpler than it may sound, and it can sometimes yield much better results than the see-also references which you find in the Library of Congress subject-heading list, especially when you are dealing with a proper-noun subject. It is always better to spend a little time getting the right subject headings than to waste a lot of time reading the wrong books.

Title entries for a book can occasionally be helpful in leading you to the precise subject heading you need. Suppose, for example, you wanted to find the subject heading for modern painting. Even with the help of see-also references, you probably would not find it. But a quick check of the author-title catalog may lead you to a book or books with the title (not a subject heading) *Modern Painting,* as for example:

---

       Modern painting.
ND     Raynal, Maurice.
195      Modern painting. [Translated by Stuart Gilbert.
R3.13   Geneva] Skira [1953]
       339 p. illus. (part col.) 35 cm.


       1. Painting. 2. Art, Modern—20th cent. 3. Painters. I. Title.

---

Having found this title entry in the author-title catalog, it is now a very simple matter for you to examine the subject headings at the bottom of the card, where you will immediately discover that the subject heading you want is "Art, Modern—20th century." You would then look in the *subject* catalog under that heading, where you would find cards for other books on modern painting, as well as further subject headings to pursue at the bottom of *those* cards. Of course this approach will not always work (if the library owns no books entitled *Modern Painting* then you must take another approach) but it is always worth trying when the more straightforward approaches have failed.

The subject catalog has certain limitations that you should know about. It gives no access at all to newspaper and periodical articles, nor to any subject that is dealt with in substantially less than book-length form. Encyclopedia articles cover an enormous range of subjects, but the subject catalog will not lead you directly to any of them. A biographical dictionary will give information about thousands of persons, but the subject catalog will not direct you to a single article in that dictionary. If an entry is to be made for a book in the subject catalog, that book must be entirely or very substantially devoted to the subject under which it is entered. The subject catalog does not make an intensive analysis of the subject content of the collection, because to do this in card-file form would lead to a catalog of undesirable physical bulk. Other devices have therefore been provided to make possible access to periodical articles and other non-book forms, and you will learn what some of these are in the next chapter.

The chief virtue of the catalog (and one worth remembering) is that it is a record of materials that the library actually owns. Printed indexes and bibliographies, which you will learn to use in conjunction with the catalog, analyze the contents of published materials in much greater depth than the library's catalog, but they constitute a record of what has been published, not necessarily of what the library owns. In them you will often find citations to publications that you would like to see but cannot, because they are not in the library. Therefore, as a matter of strategy, a usual starting point of literature searches you make as an undergraduate student will be the catalog of your library; if it fails to yield the results you desire, you would then turn to periodical and other special indexes and bibliographies for help. (As a graduate student in a library with hundreds of thousands, or even millions of books, you would reverse this process, and start with the printed bibliographies in your field, turning to the subject catalog only as a last resort.)

One final word of advice on using the subject catalog: whenever you have exhausted your own resources of imagination and judgment and still have not determined the correct subject-heading forms for a topic you are interested in, then go ask the library's professional staff for help. They will sometimes be able to suggest alternative possibilities that may not have occurred to you and will always be glad to help you after you have made a reasonable attempt to help yourself.

# 4

# Publications
# Less Than Book Length

Any search for materials in a library is complicated by the fact that there is no single bibliography that will lead you directly to all of them. Much of the universe of books is still an uncharted wilderness; and even those regions that have been carefully explored often have no comprehensive atlas to guide you through them. Part of the difficulty of providing adequate guides is simply a matter of numbers: since Gutenberg's day, some fifty million different titles have been published throughout the world, and it seems unlikely that any *single* device will ever be created that will provide easy access to the contents of all these books, or even a major portion of them. The rest of the difficulty arises from the fact that the book world is a continually expanding one, with new books and periodical articles being added to it every day—so even if a bibliography should be published today giving access to every piece of writing in existence, it would be slightly out of date tomorrow, and incomplete.

Novices typically regard the library catalog as a completely effective and self-sufficient record of a library's contents, but this is far from the truth. And even if it were, the catalog would still be a record of only a small fraction of the written materials that are in existence. The library catalog is a common starting point in a search, but it will often be no more than that, because it usually does *not* provide access to materials in the library that are published in forms substantially less than normal book length. This is a fact worth remembering whenever you begin a search for information on any subject.

If you are looking for a periodical or newspaper article, a brief biography, a book review, or plays, short stories, short poems, or essays published in collections, you will normally be unable to locate them directly in either the subject catalog or the author-title catalog, even if the library actually owns the item you are looking for. A substantial number of special bibliographies, often called indexes, have therefore been compiled to enable readers to locate such materials. With some of these you should become acquainted right away: examine *carefully* the ones discussed below and marked with a + sign, considering the ways in which they are organized and the uses to which they may be put. As occasion arises later on in your studies, you can learn about others that may be useful to you.

One way to discover what indexes are available for a particular subject or literary form is to consult the subject catalog under the name of the subject or form with the subdivision "Bibliography" or "Indexes," or both. Thus you would find an index of art entered in the subject catalog under "Art—Bibliography" and/or "Art—Periodicals—Indexes"; an index of biographies under "Biography—Bibliography" and/or "Biography—Indexes"; an index of plays under "Drama—Bibliography" and/or "Drama—Indexes," and so on. Another way is to look under the entry for indexes in the index of Constance Winchell's *Guide to Reference Books* and its supplements, where you will be led to descriptions of a great variety of indexes, some of which your library may own.

You should always remember that failure to locate desired material in the card catalog is not conclusive evidence that the library does not own that material; it simply means that it does not own it in book-length form, though it may have substantial quantities of it in shorter forms. An awareness of this fact can spare you many a fruitless search.

## PERIODICALS

The publication of materials in periodical form began, for all practical purposes, in 1665, with the appearance of the *Philosophical Transactions* of the Royal Society of London and the *Journal des Sçavans* in Amsterdam. (Both are still being published.) Since that time more than a million different periodical titles have come into being, a circumstance that has given students and librarians frequent occasion to lament, with King David, "Lord, how are they increased that trouble me!" Some means of access to the contents of this incredible outpouring was necessary, but library catalogs were unable to cope with the problem. Comprehensive printed indexes were needed, and in 1848, nearly two centuries after periodical publication began, the first one appeared: *Poole's Index to Periodical Literature,* which eventually covered the period between 1802 and 1907, indexing some 12,000 volumes of 470 American and English periodicals.

Dozens of periodical indexes have been published since Poole's pioneering venture, some of them limited to the periodical output of a single country, and others limited to the output on a single subject. A comprehensive index of the periodical literature of all nations on all subjects has never been attempted. The most comprehensive of all general indexes, the *Bibliographie der deutschen Zeitschriftenliteratur,* has indexed as many as 4,500 different periodicals at one time, but all of them were of German origin.

The principal successor to Poole's was the *Readers' Guide to Periodical Literature* (+), a general index that was begun in 1900 and is still appearing. Of the hundred thousand or more periodicals now being published the world over, the *Readers' Guide* indexes only about 125 (less than two-tenths of one percent of the total output), and all of these are published in the United States. In the front of each of its issues the *Readers' Guide* lists the titles of all the periodicals that it indexes. From a casual survey of these titles you will discover that the *Readers' Guide* will lead you generally to materials of a decidedly popular and unscholarly character. If you are looking for a scholarly article on a certain subject, the *Readers' Guide* will not give you much help.

Like most other periodical indexes, the *Readers' Guide* enables you to locate articles when you know either the author's name or the subject, but it does not give entries under title except in the case of plays and short stories. Subject entries are made under Library of Congress subject-heading forms: what you have learned about these forms in earlier exercises should therefore facilitate your use of the *Readers' Guide* and certain other periodical indexes that also use Library of Congress forms. Here is a sample subject entry from the *Readers' Guide:*

ART, French

> *Aesthetics of failure. M. Kosloff. Nation 197:*
> *202–3 O 5 '63*
> *See also*
> Dadaism

What this entry tells you is that a man named Kosloff has written an article about French art entitled "Aesthetics of Failure," which was published in volume 197 of the periodical *Nation,* on pages 202-203 of the issue dated October 5, 1963.

At the end of this citation you find a see-also reference to Dadaism (a specific school of French art), which means that you will find additional related articles entered in the index under the heading "Dadaism."

The *Social Sciences and Humanities Index*[1] (+) is similar to the *Readers' Guide* in structure and use, but the character of the periodicals that it

---

[1] In 1965 this index changed its name from the *International Index,* a far less descriptive title than its present one. Anything published serially is likely to change its title several times in the course of its life, a circumstance that can lead to some very perplexing complications whenever you are working with periodical literature.

indexes is altogether different. They are scholarly and technical, and include periodicals published in Great Britain and Canada as well as the United States. *The Readers' Guide* indexes such popular magazines as *Time, Life, The New Yorker, Good Housekeeping, Scientific American, American Artist, Yachting,* and *Ebony;* the *Social Sciences and Humanities Index* is limited to such scholarly journals as *Studies in Philology, Economic History Review, Canadian Historical Review, Philosophy of Science, Slavic Review,* and *Musical Quarterly.* Some 170 periodicals are currently covered by the *Social Sciences and Humanities Index,* most of them, as the title suggests, in the field of the humanities and the social sciences. Access to the scholarly periodical literature of the physical sciences is not possible either with the *Readers' Guide* or the *Social Sciences and Humanities Index.* Other indexes, some of which are discussed below, are available for this purpose.

In addition to the general, but very limited, coverage provided by the *Readers' Guide* and the *Social Sciences and Humanities Index,* the periodical literature of various specific subject fields is now covered by special indexes. Some 200 different periodical titles in the field of education are indexed in the *Education Index* (+); the *Art Index* (+) gives access to the periodical literature of the fine arts; and articles on business and economics can be located through the *Business Periodicals Index* (+). There are in all several hundred indexes listing more than a million periodical articles each year. As an undergraduate you will use only a few of these; but should you go on to graduate school you would then need to learn something of the indexes available in your particular field.

There is a special kind of periodical index known as an abstract, which gives, in addition to general access to periodical articles, brief summaries of the content of each article cited. The prime example of this kind of index is *Chemical Abstracts* (+), which since 1907 has been briefly summarizing articles on chemistry published in more than 10,000 different scientific periodicals. A quick look at the hundreds of volumes of *Chemical Abstracts* in the library will give you some idea of the staggering output of chemical literature and of the formidable bibliographic problems that a chemist must solve before undertaking the solution of what he thinks to be a new problem in chemistry. As with scholars in other fields, it is foolish for a chemist to engage in research on a problem that has already been solved by someone else, and the only way he can determine whether he has a really new problem on his hands is to search all the relevant literature on his problem. The chemist, like any other scholar, must therefore develop expertise in bibliography, or he is likely to find himself in the embarrassing predicament of announcing to the world a discovery that once thrilled men now long dead.

The classic case of this kind of embarrassment occurred in 1900, when biologists who were then discovering the laws governing the inheritance of plant and animal characteristics learned, to their astonishment and dismay, that a man named Mendel had already made the same discoveries several decades earlier and had published them in a periodical called the *Verhandlungen* of the Naturforschender Verein in Brunn, in the years 1865 and 1869. There they lay forgotten, with the result that what should have been a bibliographical problem (the discovery of the articles) became instead a biological problem (the rediscovery of the Mendelian laws of inheritance). The likelihood of a recurrence of this sort of thing in the field of biology has been greatly reduced in recent decades by the regular publication of a periodical index called *Biological Abstracts,* which does for the biological sciences what *Chemical Abstracts* does for chemistry.

Periodical abstracts are also published in fields other than chemistry and biology (e.g. *Abstracts of English Studies* and *Science Abstracts).* Should you wish to learn what they are, you could consult the subject catalog of a library that owns them, Winchell's *Guide to Reference Books* (+), or an expert in your field of interest.

In using any periodical index, you should always consider the extent of its coverage (that is, the number of periodicals it indexes), the character of its coverage (scholarly or popular), and its subject range (general, as in the case of the *Readers' Guide;* limited, as in the case of the *Social Sciences and Humanities Index;* or highly specialized, as in the case of *Chemical Abstracts).* Since all periodical indexes are restricted (some very severely) in the extent, character, or range of their coverage, it follows that you should always be aware of their restrictions when using them.

You will discover as you begin to make use of periodical indexes that they are no better than the library you are using them in. These indexes comprise a record of what has been published in periodicals, but they are not necessarily a record of what is actually in the library. In a library whose periodical collection is weak you may not find on the shelves more than five or ten percent of the articles cited in an index. Searching for periodical literature is therefore inevitably a more difficult task than searching for books in the library's catalog (which is a record of materials that the library actually owns), and always calls for patience and perseverance.

Why bother to consult the periodical literature of a subject when you can often find information about it more easily in a book? The principal reason is that the current periodical literature will normally contain information that is far more recent than the information you will find in a book. A scholarly perodical article will usually contain information that is only several months to a year out of date on the day the article is published. But information in a book will ordinarily be at least several years out of date when the book is published, because of the time that is required for the writer to research his subject, write it up, find a publisher, and get the book printed. Whenever recentness is a prime concern, periodical literature will be a principal source of information. When something even more recent than periodical literature is required, you might write a letter to a scholar who is known to be an expert in the subject, or search the recent issues of a newspaper that is comprehensive in its coverage. And, of course, there will always be valuable material to be found even in very old periodicals, material which never gets published in any other form. Some writings, like most wines, improve with age.

## NEWSPAPERS

A great newspaper such as the *New York Times,* which attempts to give adequate coverage of all areas of human endeavor—political, scientific, social, artistic, literary, musical, athletic, educational, recreational—can often be an excellent source of research materials, and may sometimes be the only source available. If you are not yet acquainted with the *Times* (which has been publishing since 1851), you should try reading it regularly for a week; then if you give it up, the judgment will go against you as a reader, rather than the *Times* as a newspaper. Not only does it have something of value for every enlightened reader, or every reader seeking enlightenment, it is also a model of expository prose style from which any writer can learn the standards of excellence in contemporary English prose. It is an excellent research source in almost any field you might choose to investigate, and should therefore never be overlooked in the course of a literature search. For local history, of course, you will usually have to turn to local newspapers, but otherwise the *Times* would commonly be your principal newspaper source.

In addition to all its other virtues, the *Times* periodically publishes a comprehensive index of its contents, enabling you to locate readily a vast amount of information that you may not be able to find anywhere else. Even if the *Times's* coverage of a particular event is inadequate for your purposes, you can at least determine from the index precisely when the event took place, and this can be extremely helpful in tracing the information in some other source. Suppose, for example, you were making a study of some minor Indianapolis political figure and found several very brief facts about his activities in the *New York Times.* Having established in this way the dates of these activities, it would then be a very simple matter to locate Indianapolis newspapers published on those dates, where you might reasonably expect to find far more extensive information about your man than the *Times* was willing to provide.

Your library probably owns extensive back-files of the *Times* on microfilm, as well as the indexes to them, so you have the opportunity to learn early in your academic career how to work with that most uncongenial of bibliographical forms, the microfilm reel. This form is essentially a regression to the ancient and unwieldy book-form, the scroll, which gave way to the leaf form of the book in the latter days of the Roman Empire, when the use of parchment (which can be stitched) made possible the binding together of leaves in the book-form as we now know it. Like the scroll, the microfilm reel must be unrolled as it is read and re-rolled before it can be read again. To locate any particular page on the reel, you must roll your way there, and then back again. Spot-checking a number of pages from index entries can be a tedious task with a microfilm reel. In this respect, the microfilm form of the book represents a distinct advance backwards.

If your library does not own back-files of the *New York Times,* it will probably have a complete set of the publication *Facts on File: World News Digest with Index.* First published in 1940, it is issued weekly. While its coverage is not nearly so comprehensive as that of the *Times,* it makes a very satisfactory substitute if the *Times* is not available.

## BIOGRAPHIES

Biographical information is very easily found in a library when the library happens to own a full-length biography of the individual in question: you simply look in the subject catalog under the name of the biographee, and there you will find an entry for the book you need. But it often happens that the library owns no book-length biography of the man you are interested in, and you will then find no entry for him in the subject catalog. In this event there are two courses open to you.

You might first consult a general encyclopedia or an appropriate biographical dictionary to see if your man is listed there. A large library will own many biographical dictionaries, and this raises the problem of determining which one is most likely to have the information you need. The subject catalog can be helpful here. If you need biographical details about an American historical figure, you could look in the subject catalog under the heading "U. S.—Biography—Dictionaries" and find the location of dictionaries of American biography. Or if you know your classification outline well enough, you could proceed directly to the reference collection (where most biographical dictionaries are shelved), survey the books in Class E (U. S. history and biography),[2] and soon locate all the dictionaries of American biography that the library owns. If the man you are interested in is a chemist, and you know this much at the start, you might then look under the heading "Chemists" in the subject catalog to see what biographical dictionaries of chemists the library may own. Or, again, if you knew your classification outline, you could go directly to the reference shelf and look for a biographical dictionary in Class QD (chemistry).[3] Biographical dictionaries of authors are entered in the subject catalog under

---

[2] This is a Library of Congress class designation. In the Dewey Decimal System, the book might be shelved somewhere in class 920 (biography) or under some other special designation used in your local library.

[3] The Dewey number for the same class would probably be 925 or 926.

such headings as "Authors, American," "Authors, English," "Authors, French," and so on. General biographical dictionaries having no specific national or subject focus are entered under the heading "Biography—Dictionaries."

If after consulting all the relevant biographical dictionaries, you still have not found the information you want, there is yet another direction you may take. Biographical essays often appear both in periodical articles and as chapters in books of collective biography, but the subject catalog gives access to neither of these forms. To locate these essays, you have only to consult a work called the *Biography Index* (+) which annually lists sources of information for some ten thousand individuals, both living and dead. Under the name of a biographee in the *Biography Index* you will find listed the titles of books and periodical articles in which biographical information has appeared. To give you some idea of the scope of the work, the *Biography Index* between 1946 and 1961 listed some hundred and sixty different essays and articles about Albert Schweitzer alone and each year continues to list ten or fifteen pieces about him. The *Biography Index* regularly cites biographical information appearing in more than 1,500 different periodicals (including newspaper obituaries and the like), as well as analyzing each year the biographical contents of several hundred books of collective biography. As a bibliography of ancient and modern biography it has few rivals, but like all other indexes and bibliographies, it is no better than the library it is being used in. It is only a record of what has been published, and this of course leaves you with the problem of determining which of the items published is actually available in the library.

In addition to the *Biography Index,* you may also wish to consult the various periodical indexes (*Readers' Guide,* etc.) and the *New York Times Index* to locate sources of information which may not have been recorded in the *Biography Index.*

## BOOK REVIEWS

There will be times when you want a professional critic's estimate of a book you are reading, or are about to read, and this means you will want to read one or more reviews of the book. How do you find these reviews? One way is to look in a periodically published work called the *Book Review Digest* (+), which each year gives brief digests of the reviews of some 3,000 new books in the English language. In addition to the list of digests that is given under the author's name, there is a title and subject index that enables you to identify books when you do not have the author's name. The source of each review is fully specified, so if you are not content with reading the digest you can find the periodical in which the review appeared and read the whole thing there. The longer reviews often present expert synoptic views of the subject treated in the book, along with recommendations of other books in the same area, and will sometimes give you an excellent introduction to an unfamiliar subject as well as a criticism of the book.

Of the various publications in which book reviews regularly appear, one you should know intimately is the *Times Literary Supplement* (+), an English weekly that is noted for the formidable (but lucid) scholarship of its reviewers. Since the reviewers are always anonymous, they may speak with complete candor about the shortcomings of the books they review. The worth of a book that weathers a *TLS* review unscathed is open to very little doubt. Besides the reviews, which cover books in numerous fields, the *TLS* also includes articles and commentary on the cultural scene in general. And for readers who appreciate the art of civilized invective, the "Letters to the Editor" section of the *TLS* regularly exhibits that art in its most highly developed form. Anyone who believes that the affairs of scholarship are necessarily sedate or dry-as-dust will find a sure corrective for his mistaken view in the fiery letters published by the *TLS*.

## PLAYS, SHORT STORIES, AND POEMS

Plays by various authors will often be collected and published together in a single book. Such a book will usually have an editor—the man who decided which plays would be included, and prepared their texts for publication— and the entries in the author-title catalog will be under the *editor's* name and the title of the collection. There will ordinarily be no entry for the names of the individual playwrights whose plays are in the book, nor will there be title entries for their plays. Hence you will not be able to locate directly in the catalog an individual play published in a collection of plays.

Suppose you wanted to read Jean Anouilh's play *The Lark,* and went to the catalog and found no books entered there under Anouilh's name. You might well conclude from this fact that the library owned no copy of the play. You could be wrong. For the play might be in the library in an anthology of twenty plays by various authors, edited by John Gassner and entitled *Twenty Best European Plays on the American Stage.* How do you discover this when the catalog gives you no help? You have only to consult one of the several play indexes in the library. In the *Play Index, 1953-1960* (+), you will find the following entry (here given in part):

Anouilh, Jean . . .
   The lark; adapted by Lillian Hellman . . .
   *In* Gassner, J. ed. Twenty best European plays
     on the American stage
   *In* A treasury of the theatre

This entry tells you that a play called *The Lark,* written by Jean Anouilh and adapted by Lillian Hellman, can be found in a collection of plays edited by J. Gassner entitled *Twenty Best European Plays on the*

*American Stage,* and in another collection also edited by Gassner, with the title *A Treasury of the Theatre.* Having thus identified two collections in which *The Lark* has been published, you can then check the catalog to see whether the library has them. If it does not, then you will have to check other play indexes to see if you can come up with other collections containing *The Lark* that the library may own. Play indexes usually give entries under title as well as author, so if you remember the title of a play but have forgotten the author's name, you can still locate it. Some play indexes also list plays by subject. Should you want to find a play on the subject of communism, for example, you could look in the *Play Index* under the heading "Communism" and find about a dozen. The various play indexes that your library may own can be found through the subject catalog under the subject heading "Drama—Bibliography."

Like plays, short stories are often published in collections containing the work of various authors, brought together and edited by one person. Catalog entry for these collections will be made only under the editor's name, the title of the collection, and the subject "Short stories," so access to individual stories will be possible only through indexes similar in organization and use to the ones discussed above for plays. Entries in the indexes are made under the names of authors of individual stories, under titles, and under subjects. Under the author entries you will find listed the titles of collections in which the author's stories have been published. The title and subject entries will refer you to the main listing under the author's name. Short-story indexes that your library owns will be listed in the subject catalog under the heading "Short stories—Bibliography."

The principal index to poems in collections is Granger's *Index to Poetry* (+), which gives access to the poems in more than five hundred different anthologies. If you know the name of the author, or the title, or the first line of almost any poem ever anthologized in the English language, you will be able to find it by using Granger. In it you will also find a subject index, so if you want to read a poem about socialism or capitalism or communism or concentration camps or dawn or death or eels or elephants or germs or ghosts or gnus or whatever, you can find it with ease. Often in writing term papers you will be stuck for want of fresh ideas, and will need something to jog your imagination into activity. Reading a short poem on the subject you are treating will sometimes serve this purpose passing well, suggesting to you fresh insights into the subject and angles of approach to it that may not have occurred to you. To find the appropriate poem, you would of course use the subject index in Granger.

## ESSAYS AND CHAPTER-LENGTH WRITINGS

In chapter 26 of John Gassner's *Masters of the Drama,* you will find an excellent essay on the Russian playwright Maxim Gorky. Gassner's book is entered in the subject catalog under two headings: "Drama—History and criticism" and "Dramatists," these very general headings being used because the book as a whole is not confined to the drama of any nation or period, nor to the work of any one dramatist. It deals with the drama and dramatists of all periods.

Now suppose you are writing a paper on Gorky and wish to find some information about him. You might first consult a general encyclopedia, or a special dictionary of the drama, or an appropriate biographical dictionary for some highly condensed introductory information on the topic, and then you might turn to the subject catalog to see what books you could find under suitable subject headings. Let us suppose that you looked first under the heading "Gorky, Maxim," and found nothing, and then tried "Russian drama" and "Dramatists, Russian" with equally bad results. You might then conclude that your only recourse would be to periodical literature, since the catalog had given negative results. But Gassner's book with the chapter on Gorky is in the library, although it is entered under subject headings of such a general nature that it may not occur to you even to consider them.

How then do you discover Gassner's essay on Gorky? What you need is a bibliography of some kind that analyzes the contents of books in greater depth than the subject catalog does, and an extremely useful bibliography called the *Essay and General Literature Index* (+) is available for this purpose. In the volume covering books published between 1934 and 1940, you will find the following entry:

Pieshkov, Aleksiei Maksimovich [Gorky's real name]
  Gassner, J. W. Maxim Gorky and the Soviet drama
  *In* Masters of the drama, p525-41

Having learned from this entry that Gassner's book *Masters of the Drama* contains an essay on Gorky, you would then go to the author-title catalog to see whether the library owns Gassner's book, and, if so, where it is shelved. (Since the *Essay and General Literature Index* is issued on a continuing basis and is already in more than five volumes, covering the period from 1900 to the present, you would naturally want to check all the volumes if you were undertaking a fairly comprehensive search for materials.)

The *Index* is by no means limited to works on drama. It indexes books on all other forms of *belles lettres,* historical and biographical works; books on political science, sociology, and economics; philosophical and religious writings; and certain kinds of books in the physical sciences. It is a monumental general bibliography that can be extremely useful to you in almost any kind of information search. Each year it indexes thousands of essays that cannot be easily located in a library catalog even when the library owns the books in which the essays were published. It deserves your special attention as a bibliographical tool that sometimes rivals the catalog itself in general usefulness.

## SUBJECT BIBLIOGRAPHIES

Printed bibliographies of a subject will often list not only whole books dealing with the subject, but also periodical articles and essays, to which the subject catalog gives no access. A subject bibliography may therefore perform simultaneously the function of both the subject catalog and the periodical index. Another of its virtues is that it will usually cite some items not owned by your library, but which you may wish to see anyhow. Having learned of their existence from the bibliography, you can set about the task of getting them into your hands, either by buying them yourself, asking your library to buy them, or borrowing them from some other library.

While you may seldom make use of subject bibliographies as an undergraduate, relying instead on the library's catalog and the various indexes mentioned above, it is not too early for you to examine some specimens and consider the uses to which they might be put. Here are several examples:

Bateson, F. W. (ed.). *The Cambridge Bibliography of English Literature.* 5 vols. Cambridge: The University Press, 1940-57.

Borton, Hugh; Elisseeff, Serge; and Reischauer, Edwin O. (comps.). *A Selected List of Books and Articles on Japan, in English, French, and German.* Washington: Committee on Japanese Studies, American Council of Learned Societies, 1940.

Kennedy, Arthur G. *A Bibliography of Writings on the English Language, from the Beginning of Printing to the End of 1922.* New York: Hafner Publishing Co., 1961.

Read, Conyers (ed.). *Bibliography of British History, Tudor Period, 1485-1603.* Oxford: The Clarendon Press, 1959.

Smith, Gordon Ross. *A Classified Shakespeare Bibliography, 1936-1958.* University Park: Pennsylvania State University Press, 1963.

A concluding reminder and caveat: printed bibliographies, indexes, and abstracts are records of what has been published, but not necessarily of what the library owns. This means that you must always take at least two steps in using any of them. First, you determine from these bibliographies what has been published on your topic; then, you check the catalog to see what the library owns of the things that have been published. This is cumbersome, but it is the only way to avail yourself of the deeper analysis of the contents of the library that bibliographies and indexes afford.

The great merit of using the library's catalog directly is that it saves you one step in your search; but it has the defect of providing direct access only to the contents of whole books. In any extensive search for information you will therefore use both the catalog and whatever printed bibliographies and indexes are available, drawing on the merits of both and thereby offsetting their individual deficiencies. Since the catalog is a record of what is actually available, it is usually good strategy to begin your search there, as you may be able to find directly in it all the material you need. If more information were required than the catalog led you to, you would then turn to the indexes and other bibliographies that the library owns.

# 5

# Classification of Books

Classification is the systematic arrangement of objects or ideas on the basis of some feature or features that they possess in common. We classify for the purpose of making things easier to grasp intellectually or manage physically. Biologists classify living things in order to understand the relationships between them; draft boards classify young men in order to know the size and characteristics of the available military force. Postmen classify mail according to its contents and manner of delivery; and grocers arrange their stock on principles that housewives can understand, and bachelors cannot.

Librarians classify books either for their own convenience, for the convenience of their patrons, or both. In some libraries whose stacks are closed to the public, the books will be classified by size, with all books ten inches high shelved in one place, all books eleven inches high in another, and so on, the purpose being to make the maximum use of the available shelf space. In such a library a book on mathematics might be shelved between a book on art and one on religion, if they were all the same height. Books might also be classified and arranged on the shelves according to the color of their bindings, though this arrangement would probably please no one except an interior decorator.

Classification by date of publication is another possibility, and this basis is in fact used in some special library collections whose purpose is to illustrate the historical development of the art of printing. Books may be classified by the language in which they are written, with all German books in one section, French in another, and so on, and public libraries in large cities may employ just such a system of classification for the convenience of the various ethnic groups who use the library.

Another possibility of arrangement, which is seldom used except perhaps in small private collections, is to place books on the shelves in the alphabetical order of their authors' names. Your immediate impression may be that this is the best of all possible ways to arrange books, since it would permit you to walk directly to the shelves and locate any book whose author's name you knew, without stopping by the catalog to find its call number. (Strictly speaking, this is not a *classified* order: it is alphabetical, and the alphabet is a conventional, not a logical, sequence of elements.) The disadvantage of an alphabetical arrangement is that it scatters books which have some logical relationship to each other, and places side by side books that have nothing in common. If in an alphabetically arranged collection you wished to examine a number of books on mathematics, you would have to walk through the entire library to find them, and in a large library this could mean a walk of several miles.

In most American libraries with open-stack collections, books are classified on the basis of their subject content. The purpose is to bring together on the shelves, for the convenience of readers and librarians, all the books that the library owns on a given subject. Ideally (and classification, like all human endeavors, is never ideal) all books on the Civil War would stand side by side on a library's shelves, so that if you were able to find one book on the Civil War in the library, you would have at once found them all. But writers of books seldom confine themselves to a single topic; often they do not choose to, and often the nature of their subject forbids them to do so. A man who sets out to write an economic history of the Civil War must inevitably write a good deal about the Civil War in general as he writes about its economic history, and his finished book poses this problem to a classifier in a library: Shall I class this book with other books on the Civil War or with other books on economic history? Whatever his decision, it is bound to please some persons and bother others. If a man writes a history of banking systems in New York during the mid-nineteenth century, should it be classed with other books on banking, with histories of the Jacksonian era, or with histories of New York? There is no ideal solution to such a problem, since one book cannot be shelved in three different places at the same time, so a realistic compromise is reached by shelving the book according to the subject that appears to receive the greatest emphasis in the book. This means that shelf classification of books is something less than one hundred percent efficient in bringing together on the shelves all books on a given topic; but half a loaf is better than none, provided you know what use to make of that half that has been prepared for you.

Proper use of a shelf-classification system will reveal to you much of a library's resources on a given topic, directly, in the books themselves as they stand before you on the shelves, where their contents can be conveniently inspected. What you fail to find directly on the shelves can of course be found indirectly by consulting both the catalog and a variety of bibliographies, dictionaries, indexes and encyclopedias. Rightly regarded, classification can be a great convenience to users of a library, in spite of the fact that it will never answer all the needs of a literature search.

Various systems for classifying books have been developed over the centuries, but only two have been widely used in this country: the Dewey, and the Library of Congress system. The latter system is so named because it was developed by the Library of Congress (in Washington, D. C.) for use in its own collection, which now exceeds twelve million volumes. The system was developed over a period of several decades (beginning around 1900) and represents the joint effort of dozens of scholars working with hundreds of thousands of books. The result is one of the monumental scholarly achievements of our time. That it is monumental you can determine at a glance, for the schedules (that is, the outlines of the various subject areas with the class numbers that have been assigned to them) occupy more than twenty volumes, some of them quite large.

The Library of Congress system divides the world of knowledge into twenty-one major parts, each designated by a single capital letter. Thus, for example, the letter A has been assigned to the class of general works (encyclopedias and the like, which cover all subjects); H to the social sciences; M to music; P to languages and literature; and Z to bibliography. Most of these major classes are further divided into subclasses by the addition of a second letter, these subclasses are further divided by the addition of numerals, and in some cases a finer division is accomplished by a letter-number addition to the numerals. In the schedule for class H, to cite a single example, you will find in the preliminary pages a complete synopsis of the class, beginning as follows:

| | |
|---|---|
| H | General works |
| HA | Statistics |
| HB | Economic theory |
| HC-HD | Economic history |
| HE | Transportation and communication |

and so on through class HX: Socialism, Communism, Anarchism. Following this synopsis, a complete outline of the divisions of each of these subclasses is given. Under subclass HA, Statistics, the subdivisions are outlined like this:

HA
| | |
|---|---|
| 1—23 | General [i.e., any book bearing the class number HA 1, HA 2, HA 3...HA 23 will deal with some aspect of the subject of statistics in general.] |
| 29—33 | Theory. Method. |
| 35 | Study and teaching [and so on.] |

Finally, in the main body of the schedule itself, you will find the complete record of all divisions of all classes. For instance, the class number for statistics of North Carolina is HA 551; for South Carolina, HA 621; for Russia, HA 1431; for the Ukraine, HA 1448.U6. At the back of each schedule there is an alphabetical index of subjects which will lead you to their sequential position in the classification schedule. Should you wish to find the class number for books on advertising, you might look under the term "advertising" in the index, where you would find the entry "Advertising: HF 5801-6181," and under it the various topical subdivisions of advertising with their corresponding class numbers.

This is one method of finding the class number of a given subject, but you will probably not often use it unless you are making a fairly comprehensive search for the literature of a particular subject. Another way, less cumbersome and also less reliable, is to consult the subject catalog. Suppose you found ten cards with the subject heading "League of Nations," and eight of those cards had call numbers beginning JX 1975. It would then be a fair inference that JX 1975 was the class number for books about the League of Nations, and if you wished to verify this inference, you could do so by checking the number in the classification schedules. What about those other two cards which began with some number other than JX 1975? These evidently represent books whose major emphasis is on some other subject, although they deal tangentially, or secondarily, with the League of Nations and are therefore entered under that subject heading in the subject catalog.[1]

The simplest way to make use of a subject classification system is this: when, by whatever means, you have located a book on the shelves that interests you, *always* take a look at the groups of books shelved to either side of it. These books will (in a well-developed collection) deal with the same subject as the book you found first, and may well be better suited to your purposes or may suggest aspects of the subject that had not occurred to you. Do not underestimate the value of this process because of its exceeding simplicity; it can be one of the most fruitful ways of finding the books you need and can yield many pleasant surprises. Any time you want to experience the joys of serendipity, go to the shelves and start browsing in some subject area that has caught your interest. This is called "reading the shelves," an activity that is the hallmark of a mature reader. When you

---

[1] This circumstance points up a fundamental difference between the capabilities of classification and subject cataloging: since a book can be shelved at only one place, classification can indicate only one subject for that book. But any number of subject entries can be made for the book in the subject catalog. The subject catalog gives fuller access to the subject content of books, but gives you only a catalog card to look at instead of the book itself; classification gives you limited access to the subject content of books, but allows you to stand directly before the books themselves and examine their contents briefly, while deciding which book is best suited to your purpose. Using the subject catalog is like trying to choose a wife from a Lonely Hearts Club listing: the offerings are numerous, but you have only a vague idea of what you may be getting. The classification approach to books is like choosing a wife from the girls in your home town: the offerings are limited, but you can see with your own eyes what is available.

have learned to read shelves as well as books, you have made a significant advance along the road to intellectual maturity.

Like the Library of Congress system, the Dewey classification system arranges books on the basis of their subject content, but the order of subjects is entirely different, and a different system of notation is used: thus the Library of Congress uses the letters DA for English history, while Dewey uses the numbers 942. By comparing the outlines of the two systems at the end of this chapter, you can see what the differences in plan and notation are. The principles of using the Dewey system are the same as those for using the Library of Congress system: if you wish to know the Dewey class number for any given subject, then consult the Dewey classification schedules, or, if you are in a library that employs the Dewey system, check the call numbers on several catalog cards under the appropriate subject heading. And whenever you find one book on your subject in a library that uses Dewey, check the other books to the left and right of it to see what else is available.

Many college libraries have begun to adopt the Library of Congress system in recent years, because of its superiority in various respects to Dewey, but the process of conversion is such a costly one that many others may never undertake it. Since both systems are likely to be in wide use for many years to come, scholars will need to be acquainted with the ground-plans of both. This is not as difficult as it may sound, since in a matter of a few minutes one may survey the entire outline of major classes in either system.

## CLASS NUMBERS AND CALL NUMBERS

A call number (the complete number that you find on the spines of books and in the upper-left corner of a catalog card) consists of a class number plus a book number, the latter serving to identify the author and title of a given work in a particular class. To illustrate, in class E 332 (the class of biographies of Thomas Jefferson), a library may own biographies written by Claude Bowers, Gene Lisitzky, Dumas Malone, T. E. Watson, and James Wise. The book number for each of these authors (in the same order) is B7.8, L7.7, M2.5, W3.4 and W8. The call number (i.e. class number plus book number) for each of their books is:

| [Bowers] | [Lisitzky] | [Malone] | [Watson] | [Wise] |
|----------|------------|----------|----------|--------|
| E        | E          | E        | E        | E      |
| 332      | 332        | 332      | 332      | 332    |
| B7.8     | L7.7       | M2.5     | W3.4     | W8     |

The effect of this system is to give each and every book in the library a distinctive and unique numerical identification (that is, a call number), and also to arrange all books in any particular class alphabetically by author and title. With a correct call number in hand, you can locate any book in the collection without further information as to its exact title or the precise spelling of the author's name.

## Editions

Any book of enduring popularity or interest will be republished in various editions, each differing in some respect, however minor, from all other editions. But since the essential content of the work remains constant throughout all editions, each edition should, it would seem, have the same call number as all others: it will belong in the same class as the others and will have the same book number. In order to give each edition a unique call number, therefore, the date of publication is added to the call number of the book. Among others, editions of Boswell's *Life of Samuel Johnson* were published in 1903, 1904, 1934, 1950, 1960, and 1961. Their call numbers are, in the same order:

| PR | PR | PR | PR | PR | PR |
|------|------|------|------|------|------|
| 3533 | 3533 | 3533 | 3533 | 3533 | 3533 |
| B6 | B6 | B6 | B6 | B6 | B6 |
| 1903 | 1904 | 1934 | 1950 | 1960 | 1961 |

Note that these call numbers are identical in all respects except the last line, where the various dates of publication serve to differentiate among them. When copying call numbers from catalog cards preparatory to going to the shelves for a book, you may find it a tiny point of convenience to omit an edition date when one is given, since even without it you will have no difficulty in locating the edition you want when you get to the shelves.

## Shelving Sequence of Call Numbers

A call number is a book's address: it tells you precisely where on the shelves a book will stand in relation to the thousands of other books in the library. Here are some examples illustrating most of the principles of arrangement of Library of Congress call numbers:

| P | P | P | P | PA | PB | Q |
|-----|------|------|-----|-------|---------|-----|
| 46 | 283 | 283 | 283 | 58 | 36 | 1 |
| R7 | A8.7 | B4.6 | B8 | A2.64 | R7.384 | M5 |

The first line of a call number consists of either one or two capital letters. The sequence of call numbers is first determined by the alphabetical order of these letters: thus in the example above all call numbers beginning with the single letter P come before all numbers beginning PA, PA comes before

PB, and PB before Q. When the first lines of two call numbers are identical, the one with the smaller number on the second line shelves first: P46 before P283. When the first *two* lines of two call numbers are identical, they are then placed in alphabetical order by the letters on the third line: P283A8.7 before P283B4.6. And when the first two lines and the letters on the third line are the same, then the call number having the smaller number on the third line comes first: P283B4.6 before P283B8. Note that on the third line of the first number in this example you have a decimal number, 4.6, which is smaller than the whole number 8 and therefore shelves before it since the call numbers are otherwise identical.

The letter O in a call number is of course indistinguishable from the number zero, but this will cause you no difficulty if you remember that there are never any numbers on the first line, nor any letters on the second line of a call number, and that the third line (and fourth, when there is one) usually begins with a single letter: thus in the call number

PR
2604
O5.8

there is a zero in the number on the second line, and the third line begins with the letter O.[2]

In addition to the call numbers, a special designation is used to specify the location of books in special collections, as in the following examples:

| Ref. | Per. | qF | fND |
|------|------|------|------|
| P | AP | 1608 | 2800 |
| 2830 | 2 | H3 | U6 |
| B4.9 | R3 | | |

The designation Ref. above the call number indicates that the book has been shelved in the reference collection and Per. the periodical collection. The lowercase letter q or f prefixed to a call number indicates that the book

[2] The arrangement of Library of Congress call numbers may vary from library to library. A common variant is the following pattern:

PR2604
O5.8

which you may also find written as

PR2604
.O58

with the decimal point preceding the letter O on the second line, indicating that the number 58 which follows is a decimal fraction. This is admittedly an odd place to put a decimal point (before a letter rather than a number), but it is a fairly widespread oddity. For a fuller discussion of the form of Library of Congress call numbers see Daniel Gore, "Further Observations on the Use of LC Classification," *Library Resources & Technical Services,* Vol. 10, No. 4 (Fall, 1966), 519-24.

has been shelved with a special collection of books that are too tall for the shelves in the general collection. The prefix q may be used for books between 11 and 15 inches high; f is for books over 15 inches. These particular designations may not be employed in your library, but some special designations are used in nearly all libraries, and if you are uncertain of their meaning or of the locations of the special collections, you can always ask someone on the library's staff for an explanation.

Call numbers in the Dewey system are constructed on the same principles, with a class number indicating the subject content of the book and a book number identifying the author and title of the book within any particular class:

| | | | | |
|---|---|---|---|---|
| 549.78 | 549.8 | 612.8116 | 612.8116 | 613 |
| B465p | A539 | R727t | R727t | M847 |
| | | 1939 | 1945 | |

The following outlines of the Library of Congress and Dewey systems of classification will show you in general where books on any broad subject in your library may be found. They can be especially useful to you, as you will learn in the next chapter, in locating readily a particular reference book in order to find the answer to some specific question. To determine the class number of any very specific subject, however, you will have to turn to the classification schedules themselves (as noted earlier in this chapter) or deduce the class number from entries in the subject catalog.

## OUTLINE OF THE LIBRARY OF CONGRESS CLASSIFICATION

A  GENERAL WORKS—
    POLYGRAPHY
AC  Collections
AE  Encyclopedias (General)
AG  General reference works
AI  Indexes (General)
AM  Museums
AN  Newspapers
AP  Periodicals (General)
AS  Societies. Academies
AY  Yearbooks (General)
AZ  General history of knowledge
    and learning

    PHILOSOPHY—
    PSYCHOLOGY—
    RELIGION
B  Philosophy (General)
BC  Logic
BD  Speculative philosophy

BF Psychology
BH Esthetics
BJ Ethics
BL Religions. Mythology. Free thought
BM Judaism
BP Mohammedanism
BR Christianity
BS Bible
BT Doctrinal theology
BV Practical theology
BX Denominations and sects

C AUXILIARY SCIENCES OF HISTORY (including universal biography)
CB History of civilization (General)
CC Archeology
CD Diplomatics, archives, seals
CE Chronology
CJ Numismatics
CN Epigraphy
CR Heraldry
CS Genealogy
CT Biography

HISTORY AND TOPOGRAPHY (except America)
D History (General): Europe (General)
DA Great Britain
DB Austria, Czechoslovakia, Hungary
DC France
DD Germany
DE Mediterranean region, Greco-Roman world
DF Greece
DG Italy
DH—DJ Netherlands
DK Russia, Poland, Finland
DL Scandinavia
DP Spain and Portugal
DQ Switzerland

DR   Turkey and the Balkan
      States
DS   Asia
DT   Africa
DU   Australia and Oceania
DX   Gipsies

### AMERICA

 E   America (General) and
      United States
      (General)
 F   United States (Local)
      and America except
      the United States

### GEOGRAPHY—
### ANTHROPOLOGY

 G   Geography (General);
      Atlases; Maps
GA   Mathematical geography,
      Cartography
GB   Physical geography
GC   Oceanography
GF   Anthropogeography
GN   Anthropology
GR   Folklore
GT   Manners and customs
      (General)
GV   Sports and amusements,
      Games

### SOCIAL SCIENCES

 H   General works
HA   Statistics
HB   Economic theory
HC   Economic history and
      conditions; National
      production
HD   Economic history:
      Agriculture and
      industries
HE   Transportation and
      communication
HF   Commerce
HG   Finance (General);
      Private finance
HJ   Public finance

HM   Sociology (General and
     theoretical)

HN   Social history. Social
     reform

HQ   Family. Marriage.
     Woman

HS   Societies: secret,
     benevolent, etc.: Clubs

HT   Communities. Classes.
     Races

HV   Social pathology. Social
     and public welfare.
     Criminology

HX   Socialism. Communism.
     Anarchism

### POLITICAL SCIENCE

J   Official documents

JA   General works

JC   Political theory
     *Constitutional History*
     *and Administration*

JF   General works

JK   United States

JL   British America. Latin
     America, etc.

JN   Europe

JQ   Asia, Africa, Australia,
     and Oceania

JS   Local government

JV   Colonies and colonization

JX   International law

K   LAW (in preparation)

### EDUCATION

L   Education (General)

LA   History of education

LB   Theory and practice;
     Teaching; Teacher
     training; School
     Administration

LC   Special aspects of
     education
     *Individual Universities,*
     *Colleges, Schools*

LD   United States

LE   Other American

LF  Europe
LG  Asia, Africa, Oceania
LH  University, college, and
      school magazines, etc.
LJ  Student fraternities
LT  Textbooks (Only those
      covering several
      subjects)

### MUSIC
M  Collections of music
ML  Literature of music
      (History and criticism,
      etc.)
MT  Musical instruction and
      study

### FINE ARTS
N  Fine arts (General)
NA  Architecture
NB  Sculpture
NC  Graphic arts in general
ND  Painting
NE  Engraving
NK  Art applied to industry.
      Decoration and
      ornament

### LANGUAGE AND
### LITERATURE
P  Philology and linguistics
      (General)
PA  Classical philology and
      literature
PB  General works, Celtic
      languages and
      literature
PC  Romance languages
PD  Germanic languages:
      general, Gothic,
      Scandinavian
PE  English language
PF  Dutch, Friesian, German
PG  Slavic languages and
      literature
PH  Finno-Ugrian and
      Basque languages and
      literatures

PJ  Oriental languages and
      literatures: general,
      Hamitic, Semitic

PK  Indo-Iranian languages
      and literatures; Indo-
      Aryan; Armenian,
      Caucasian

PL  Languages and literatures
      of Eastern Asia,
      Oceania, Africa

PM  Hyperborean, American
      Indian, and artificial
      languages

PN  Literary history and
      collections (General)

PQ  Romance literatures

PR  English literature

PS  American literature

PT  Teutonic literature

PZ  Fiction and juvenile
      literature in the
      English language,
      including translations
      into English

SCIENCE

Q  Science (General)

QA  Mathematics

QB  Astronomy

QC  Physics

QD  Chemistry

QE  Geology

QH  Natural history

QK  Botany

QL  Zoology

QM  Human anatomy

QP  Physiology

QR  Bacteriology

MEDICINE

R  Medicine (General)

RA  Public aspects of
      medicine; Medicine
      and the state, public
      health, etc.

RB  Pathology

RC  Internal medicine;
      Practice of medicine;
      Psychiatry

RD   Surgery
RE   Ophthalmology
RF   Otorhinolaryngology
RG   Gynecology and obstetrics
RJ   Pediatrics
RK   Dentistry
RL   Dermatology
RM   Therapeutics;
        Pharmacology
RS   Pharmacy and materia
        medica
RT   Nursing
RV   Botanic, Thomsonian,
        and eclectic medicine
RX   Homeopathy
RZ   Other systems of
        medicine


AGRICULTURE—
PLANT AND
ANIMAL INDUSTRY
S   Agriculture (General)
SB   Plant culture and
        horticulture
SD   Forestry
SF   Animal culture
SH   Fish culture and fisheries
SK   Hunting sports


TECHNOLOGY
T   Technology (General)

*Engineering and
Building Group*

TA   Engineering (General);
        Civil engineering
TC   Hydraulic engineering
TD   Sanitary and municipal
        engineering
TE   Roads and pavements
TF   Railroad engineering
        and operation
TG   Bridges and roofs
TH   Building construction;
        Fire prevention and
        extinction

*Mechanical Group*

TJ   Mechanical engineering

TK  Electrical engineering
      and industries;
      Electronics; Atomic
      power

TL  Motor vehicles; Cycles;
      Aeronautics

*Chemical Groups*

TN  Mining engineering,
      mineral industries

TP  Chemical technology

TR  Photography

*Composite Group*

TS  Manufactures

TT  Mechanic trades; Arts
      and crafts

TX  Domestic science;
      Cookbooks

MILITARY SCIENCE

U  Military science
     (General)

UA  Armies: Organization,
      distribution, etc.

UB  Administration

UC  Maintenance and
      transportation

UD  Infantry

UE  Cavalry; Armor

UF  Artillery

UG  Military engineering

UH  Other services

NAVAL SCIENCE

V  Naval science (general)

VA  Navies

VB  Administration

VC  Maintenance

VD  Seamen

VE  Marines

VF  Naval ordnance

VG  Minor services of navies

VK  Navigation; Merchant
      marine

VM  Naval architecture;
      Shipbuilding and
      marine engineering

Z  BIBLIOGRAPHY AND
    LIBRARY SCIENCE

## OUTLINE OF THE DEWEY DECIMAL CLASSIFICATION[3]
### (Sixteenth Edition)

| | |
|---|---|
| 000 | GENERAL WORKS |
| 010 | Bibliography |
| 020 | Library science |
| 030 | General encyclopedias |
| 040 | General collected essays |
| 050 | General periodicals |
| 060 | General societies |
| 070 | Newspaper journalism |
| 080 | Collected works |
| 090 | Manuscripts & rare books |
| | |
| 100 | PHILOSOPHY |
| 110 | Metaphysics |
| 120 | Metaphysical theories |
| 130 | Branches of psychology |
| 140 | Philosophical topics |
| 150 | General psychology |
| 160 | Logic |
| 170 | Ethics |
| 180 | Ancient & medieval |
| 190 | Modern philosophy |
| | |
| 200 | RELIGION |
| 210 | Natural theology |
| 220 | Bible |
| 230 | Doctrinal theology |
| 240 | Devotional & practical |
| 250 | Pastoral theology |
| 260 | Christian church |
| 270 | Christian church history |
| 280 | Christian churches & sects |
| 290 | Other religions |
| | |
| 300 | SOCIAL SCIENCES |
| 310 | Statistics |
| 320 | Political science |
| 330 | Economics |
| 340 | Law |
| 350 | Public administration |
| 360 | Social welfare |

[3] Reproduced from DEWEY Decimal Classification and Relative Index Edition 16 1958 by permission of Forest Press, Inc., owners of copyright.

370   Education
380   Public services & utilities
390   Customs & folklore

400   LANGUAGE

410   Comparative linguistics
420   English & Anglo-Saxon
430   Germanic languages
440   French, Provençal, Catalan
450   Italian, Rumanian
460   Spanish, Portuguese
470   Latin & other Italic
480   Classical & modern Greek
490   Other languages

500   PURE SCIENCE

510   Mathematics
520   Astronomy
530   Physics
540   Chemistry & allied sciences
550   Earth sciences
560   Paleontology
570   Anthropology & biology
580   Botanical sciences
590   Zoological sciences

600   TECHNOLOGY

610   Medical sciences
620   Engineering
630   Agriculture
640   Home economics
650   Business
660   Chemical technology
670   Manufactures
680   Other manufactures
690   Building construction

700   THE ARTS

710   Landscape & civic art
720   Architecture
730   Sculpture
740   Drawing & decorative arts
750   Painting
760   Prints & print making
770   Photography
780   Music
790   Recreation

800 LITERATURE

810 American literature in English
820 English and Old English
830 Germanic literature
840 French, Provençal, Catalan
850 Italian, Rumanian
860 Spanish, Portuguese
870 Latin & other Italic literatures
880 Classical & modern Greek
890 Other literatures

900 HISTORY

910 Geography, travels, description
920 Biography
930 Ancient history
940 Europe
950 Asia
960 Africa
970 North America
980 South America
990 Other parts of the world

# 6

# The Reference and Bibliography Collections

## THE REFERENCE COLLECTION

"Knowledge is of two kinds," said the redoubtable Dr. Johnson. "We know a subject ourselves, or we know where we can find information on it." One of the best ways to begin the acquisition of the latter species of knowledge is to become well acquainted with the reference and bibliography collections in your library. These, together with the catalogs of the library, are the usual starting points of any information search. Some knowledge of their organization and contents is indispensable to the efficient use of a library; and because the efficient use of the library will be indispensable to your adequate performance in many college courses, it follows that you should obtain this knowledge as soon as possible.

What is a reference book? Loosely defined, it is any book not designed for consecutive or complete reading: it is a book to which you refer, usually very briefly, for a specific bit of information or a concise introduction to a topic, ignoring the rest of its contents. For this reason, and because they are often in heavy demand, reference books do not circulate. The arrangement of their contents is commonly either alphabetical or chronological (sometimes both), a circumstance that makes the location of particular facts quite simple, but consecutive reading nearly impossible. But since the internal arrangement of reference books does not follow any one fixed pattern (even an alphabetically arranged encyclopedia may contain an alphabetical index to help you get at information not entered in the main alphabet of articles) it is always prudent to read enough of their prefaces to learn, in each case, how the book is to be used.

With some types of reference books, such as general encyclopedias and dictionaries, you are no doubt already familiar. But with others —

bibliographies, digests, concordances, indexes, gazetteers, biographical dictionaries, rhyming dictionaries, dictionaries of names, chronologies, handbooks, encyclopedias of specific subjects, etc.—you may have only the slenderest acquaintance, and must now begin to gain some familiarity. A good way to begin is to "read the shelves" in the reference and bibliography collections (most of the books, though not all, in class Z[1] are bibliographies, a type of reference book to be discussed briefly below), noting the variety and kinds of material available, and considering the internal arrangement of the books. A very useful outline of reference literature (for which you may have no immediate need, though it may later in your academic career be extremely helpful) is Constance Winchell's *Guide to Reference Books* and its supplements. Examine it carefully and remember its title and purpose, as you will almost certainly need to consult it at some future time.

Because you cannot remember all, or even many of the individual books comprising the reference collection, though you will frequently have occasion to consult them for some specific bit of information, some means of access to their contents is needed that does not make extraordinary demands upon your memory. Now the reference collection, like the rest of the library's collections, is arranged by the Library of Congress or the Dewey classification system, with whose major divisions (twenty-one in the Library of Congress, ten in Dewey) you should already be thoroughly familiar. Knowing these divisions, and being acquainted with the several kinds of books that form the reference collection, you should have little difficulty in locating on the reference shelves the exact book to answer a specific question, or to introduce you to a new subject. If, for example, you need a date or other detail of United States history, and know your classification outline, you can go directly to the reference collection and rapidly survey *all* the books in classes E and F[2] (since the number of books in any one class in the reference collection will always be quite small), and in this way you will very shortly come upon exactly the book required. But if you do not know how to use the classification outline, every time you need to use the reference collection you will first have to struggle with the subject catalog to determine what book or books might supply the answer to your question, a process both laborious and, oftentimes, unfruitful.

When you have once settled on a field of major study and your interests are focused on one or two classes of books rather than the whole world of knowledge, you might then very profitably make a closer acquaintance with *all* the reference books in your particular subject area, relying still on your knowledge of the classification outline to direct you on occasion to reference books outside your chosen specialty. As a student of

[1] The Dewey class for bibliography is 010, but the Dewey system makes provision for scattering bibliographies throughout the entire collection, so in some libraries you will not find all bibliographies shelved in one place, as they are in the Library of Congress system

[2] Dewey class 970.

literature, for example, you should have an intimate knowledge of the reference books in Class P;[3] if you are a chemistry major, you should know all the reference books in class QD;[4] and so on with other fields of knowledge.

## THE BIBLIOGRAPHY COLLECTION

A bibliography is a kind of reference book that lists books (and other written materials) by author or subject. Such a book is useful as an adjunct to the library's catalog in determining what an author has written or what has been published on a given subject. An annotated bibliography includes brief descriptive notes about the titles listed (Winchell's *Guide to Reference Books* is an annotated bibliography). Separately published bibliographies, with few exceptions, are shelved in class Z. Bibliographies of Shakespeare, for example, whether listing editions of his works or of studies written about them, are classed in Z8811-8814. (Note that all bibliographies of individuals are classed between Z8001-Z8999, in alphabetical order.) To find the class number of the bibliography of any subject, you can look for that subject in the alphabetical index at the back of the classification schedule for class Z, though this will not usually be the simplest technique for locating a subject bibliography. Ordinarily the best approach would be to look in the subject catalog under the name of the subject with the subdivision "Bibliography." Thus, under "Shakespeare, William—Bibliography," in the subject catalog, you will find entered whatever Shakespearean bibliographies the library owns.

There is a special kind of bibliography which you should give particular attention to: this is the bibliography that lists nothing but periodical or journal articles within a limited subject area. Examples of this are the *Applied Science & Technology Index,* the *Business Periodicals Index,* and the *Education Index.* Such indexes are now currently published for nearly all major subject fields, though your library may not own all of them. (If you wish to know about the others, you could find them listed and described in Winchell's *Guide.)*

In addition to the bibliographies that you find in Class Z, you will find bibliographies included in almost any scholarly work published nowadays on any subject and should never overlook these when you are searching for the literature of a given subject. Sometimes this will be the best (or the only) bibliographical information available in the library, and you must know where to look for it. Your library may own no separate bibliography of John

---

[3] Dewey class 800
[4] Dewey class 540

Dryden, for example, yet a very useful one appears between pages 247 and 255 of a book by Frank Moore entitled *The Nobler Pleasure,* which your library may own. (This fact can be ascertained either by looking through the books in the library on Dryden, or by looking at the catalog cards for those books, where a note will indicate whether a book contains a bibliography. On the catalog card for Moore's book, there is a note stating "Includes bibliography.") Bibliographies are also given at the end of many encyclopedia articles, and various scholarly journals include as a regular feature extensive bibliographies of their special subject fields.

Besides bibliographies of subjects and individuals, you should also know about national and universal bibliographies. National bibliographies are records of the publishing activity of an entire nation, and may be concerned either with current publications or the publications of past times. A good example of a current national bibliography is *Books in Print,* which attempts to list every book presently available from an American publisher, regardless of its date of publication; related to it is the *Cumulative Book Index,* whose monthly issues list every book published in English during the year. An outstanding example of a retrospective national bibliography is Charles Evans's *American Bibliography,*[5] in which Evans has tried to record every book, pamphlet, and periodical published in the United States from the beginning of printing in this country (1639) through the year 1800. The bibliography arranges books according to the year in which they were published, and sub-arranges them alphabetically by author. It is therefore possible to determine readily the number of titles that were published in any one year and the topics that were popular in that year. Anyone interested in the study of American history or civilization will of course find such a work indispensable.

Universal bibliographies are listings of books without any restrictions as to author, subject, language, or place of publication. Most library catalogs fall into this category, whether in card or printed book form. Of the latter, the most comprehensive of all is the catalog of the Library of Congress and its continuation, the *National Union Catalog.* This bibliography, now

---

[5] Evans is one of the most interesting figures in the history of American libraries. A bibliographer of unusual energy and ability, he held five professional posts as a librarian and was fired from all of them. He has the further distinction of having been fired from the same job twice, a thing virtually unheard of in the library profession, or any other, for that matter. Evans is responsible for the fact that on every Library of Congress catalog card the height of the book is recorded; but Melvil Dewey is responsible for the fact that the height is given in centimeters, rather than inches, so the information is meaningless to most American readers. At the first meeting of the American Library Association (1876) Evans presented a paper contending that a catalog entry for a book should always record its height, because that is a fact of considerable value to bibliographers. A committee was appointed to consider the matter, and while some of its members were out smoking, Dewey rammed through *his* proposal that the height be recorded, but in centimeters, since he felt that that whole world would soon adopt the metric system. When it does, the American library profession, having capitulated to Dewey's demands, will have a headstart on everybody else in North America.

exceeding four hundred volumes, records some ten million books, listing them by author only. Because of its vast scope, it is often very useful in identifying books and authors, and you should acquaint yourself with it. Two similar works are the British Museum catalog and the catalog of the Bibliothèque Nationale in Paris.

One other kind of bibliography you should know about: this is one which lists not titles of various books either by certain authors or about certain topics, but only titles of bibliographies. Such a bibliography is therefore called a bibliography of bibliographies, and there are definite indications that in the not very distant future we will also have to contend with many bibliographies of bibliographies of bibliographies. This series, as you can see, is capable of indefinite extension, and no one can really foresee the end of it. One bibliography of bibliographies you should be familiar with is the *Bibliographic Index,* which is a continuing record of bibliographies in all fields, including bibliographies that appear in journal articles and as part of the scholarly apparatus of individual books. Another is Theodore Besterman's *A World Bibliography of Bibliographies,* which in its fourth edition lists some 117,000 bibliographies covering all subject areas.

There is, finally, one very specialized type of bibliography that will prove invaluable to you, once you have settled upon a subject field of major interest and begun to acquaint yourself with the organization and contents of its literature. This is the bibliography that establishes the major outlines of the literature of a special field. It is commonly called "a guide to the literature." It will specify the principal periodicals, bibliographies, and reference books in each division of the field, usually giving brief descriptions of each item cited and pointing out any particular virtues or defects. The more elaborate guides will also discuss at length the most efficient procedures for conducting a literature search within the designated subject field and will sometimes give instructions on special problems of form for citations in bibliographies and footnotes. While you will have little need of such guides for the next year or so, it is not too early now to learn of their existence so you will know how and where to find them when you do need them. The two principal guides to these guides are Winchell's *Guide to Reference Books* (mentioned above) and Robert L. Collison's *Bibliographies, Subject and National: A Guide to Their Contents, Arrangement, and Use* (New York: Hafner, 1962). Listed below are some examples of guides to the literature of particular subject fields:

American Historical Association. *Guide to Historical Literature.* New York: Macmillan, 1963.
Bond, Donald F. *Reference Guide to English Studies.* 2nd ed. Chicago: University of Chicago Press, 1971.
Chamberlin, Mary W. *Guide to Art Reference Books.* Chicago: American Library Association, 1959.

Duckles, Vincent Harris. *Music Reference and Research Materials: An Annotated Bibliography.* 2nd ed. New York: Free Press, 1967.

Gohdes, Clarence. *Bibliographical Guide to the Study of the Literature of the U.S.A.* 3rd ed. Durham: Duke University Press, 1970.

Handlin, Oscar, *et al. Harvard Guide to American History.* Cambridge, Mass.: The Belknap Press of Harvard University Press, 1963.

Lewis, Peter R. *The Literature of the Social Sciences: An Introductory Survey and Guide.* London: Library Association, 1960.

Lock, C. Muriel. *Geography: A Reference Handbook.* London: Bingley, 1969.

Mellon, M. G. *Chemical Publications: Their Nature and Use.* 4th ed. New York: McGraw-Hill, 1965.

Paetow, Louis John. *A Guide to the Study of Medieval History.* Revised ed. New York: Kraus Reprint Corp., 1959.

Palfrey, Thomas Rossman. *A Bibliographical Guide to the Romance Languages and Literatures.* 3rd ed. Evanston, Ill.: Chandler, 1947.

Parke, Nathan Grier. *Guide to the Literature of Mathematics and Physics, Including Related Works on Engineering Science.* Revised ed. New York: Dover Publications, 1958.

Smith, Roger Cletus, and Painter, Reginald H. *Guide to the Literature of the Zoological Sciences.* 7th ed. Minneapolis: Burgess, 1967.

Surrency, Erwin C.; Feld, Benjamin; and Crea, Joseph. *A Guide to Legal Research.* Supplemented ed. Dobbs Ferry, N.Y.: Oceana, 1966.

Whitford, R. H. *Physics Literature: A Reference Manual.* 2nd ed. Metuchen, N. J.: Scarecrow Press, 1968.

"Of making many books," the Preacher's commentator wearily observed three thousand years ago, "there is no end." And he had scarcely witnessed the beginning. Today he might well lament, "Of making many bibliographies, there is no end." But without the system of bibliographies that has been developed to mark the routes through the growing wilderness of publications, the situation would be both wearisome and desperate. Bibliographies have become as indispensable to scholars as charts to navigators, or maps to explorers. Like road signs, they can make rather dull reading, but they may lead you to some very pleasant destinations that could never be reached without them. Once you have learned to use them efficiently, you will be able to venture alone into any of the provinces of learning that your own curiosity may impel you to enter.

# 7

# The Alphabet and Filing

Failure to locate a desired entry in the catalog can be attributed to one of three causes: (1) the entry isn't there to be found; (2) you have the wrong form of the entry; or (3) it was there but you looked for it in the wrong place. One cure for the last cause of failure (which is far more common than catalog users suspect, for they naturally assign their failures to the first cause) is to learn several of the major principles of alphabetic arrangement. (There are numerous exotic rules of filing that will not be discussed here. But if you want to see some, your librarian can show you his local set of filing rules.)

1. Entries may be arranged word by word, the alphabeting proceeding letter by letter to the end of each word. This is the principle followed in most library catalogs. But some catalogs and book indexes follow the practice of alphabeting letter by letter without regard to the end of a word, a practice which results in an arrangement of entries quite different from that usually found in library catalogs. A simple illustration will help to clarify:

| *Word-by-Word Filing* | *Letter-by-Letter Filing* |
|---|---|
| New Amsterdam | New Amsterdam |
| New Mexico | Newark |
| New York | New Mexico |
| Newark | Newton, Isaac |
| Newton, Isaac | New York |

The underlying assumption of word-by-word filing is that the alphabet consists of twenty-seven elements, the first of which is a blank space. This alphabet is therefore recited "Blank, A, B, C . . .," and a blank space always files before the letter A. Thus NewBlankYork files before Newark. The effect of word-by-word filing is, as you can see, to keep together in straight sequence in the catalog all entries beginning with the same word (or words), whereas letter-by-letter filing disperses them. If you should forget that this is the principle of filing used in a library catalog and try to find "Newark" by looking somewhere between "New Amsterdam" and "New York," you would be defeated by your own forgetfulness. Or if you should look in the index of the *Encyclopaedia Britannica* for "Newark" between "New York" and "Newton, Isaac," you would fail to find it because entries in that encyclopedia are filed letter by letter.

There is one exception in most catalogs to the word-by-word principle of filing: names that begin with a separated prefix are filed letter by letter, as if they were one word. Thus De La Mare is filed as if it were written Delamare (without spaces), Van der Bilt as Vanderbilt. This exception is intended to be a convenience to readers, who will often not know just which form—spaced or unspaced—such a name will take, but it may prove bothersome if you should forget it.

2. When the same word or phrase is used as a surname, as a place name, and as the title of a book, the personal name will file first, the place name second, and the title last:

> Reading, Geoffrey.
> Reading, England.
> Reading: A Vice or Virtue?

3. If the first word in a *title* entry is an article (*a, an,* or *the,* and their equivalents in other languages) the entry is filed by the first word in the title *following* the article. But articles occurring *after* the first word of a title are filed as any other word would be.

> The first professional revolutionist.
> First questions on marine biology.
> First questions on the life of the spirit.

4. Names.

A. Entries for persons having the same name are divided into three groups and may be filed in this order (but not by all libraries):

> Personal names with Roman numerals;
> Persons having only one name and no numerals;
> Persons with given names or initials.
> Example: Alexander I, King of Serbia.
> Alexander, Grand Duke of Russia.
> Alexander, George.

Note that a person's title (Mr., Miss, King, Queen, Margrave, Duke, Count, etc.) is normally disregarded for filing purposes, unless it is the beginning of an entry for the title of a book. When two persons have identical names, the person born first will be filed first.

B. A personal name entry in the catalog will normally consist of the family name plus the forenames in full, and often a date of birth and death as further identification.

> Jones, Daniel, 1881-
> Jones, David Edwards, 1924-
> Jones, Eli Stanley, 1884-1962.

While this is the most satisfactory identification that can be given, it can lead to some unexpected difficulties in spite of the fullness of the entry. Suppose you are searching the catalog for an author whose name usually appears on title pages of his books as D. E. Jones, and the citation you have in hand is to that form of the name. The catalog you are searching in contains the following entries, with dozens of books entered under each name:

> Jones, D. E., 1928-
> Jones, D. E., 1932-
> Jones, D. Ethelbert, 1856-1915.
> Jones, Dagobert Evans, 1898-
> Jones, David Edward, 1915-
> Jones, Delancy Egbert, 1820-1897.
> Jones, Digby Egerton, 1925-
> Jones, Donald Edward.
> Jones, Donald Edward, 1845-1920.
> Jones, Donald Edward, 1846-1918.
> Jones, Dunlap Ewart, 1820-1876.
> Jones, Dylan Easterling, 1932-1963.

It will not be an easy matter to decide which (if any) of these Joneses is the author you are looking for. If you know the title of the book by D. E. Jones, you might look for a title entry in the catalog rather than the name, which in this situation is evidently ambiguous. Or if you know something about your author's dates, or the subject that he usually wrote about, you might with these facts be able to spot the Jones you are interested in.

A different problem arises when you have in hand the full name of the author, but the cataloger has entered him under his initials, not being able to determine the full forms. Suppose the name you had in hand was Daniel Edgar Jones. His name appears to be missing from the above list, but he may well be there, disguised as either of the D. E. Joneses appearing at the head of the list. To solve this problem you could either check the titles under the two D. E. Joneses to see if the one you are interested in is there, or look instead for a title entry in the catalog.

Note that in the filing of forenames that consist only of an initial letter, the initial files before all other names beginning with the same letter, as with the Joneses above.

There is, finally, the problem that arises when you *think* you know an author's first name, but actually it is the middle name instead. Somerset Maugham, the famous British novelist, is generally referred to by his middle name Somerset, rather than his first name, which is William. If you looked in the catalog for "Maugham, Somerset," you would probably find nothing, as the cataloger has entered his books under "Maugham, William Somerset," and made no cross reference to that form from his middle name.

Because of these various difficulties in locating a name in the catalog even when you know the name in complete or nearly complete form, it is usually good strategy to look for a book under its title entry whenever you fail to find it under the author's name. Conversely, if you begin your search with a title entry and find nothing, it is a good idea then to check under the author's name if you have it, since title entries, for one reason or another, are not made for *all* books (though they are made for most of them). Title entries are never made for titles which are meaningless unless accompanied by their author's name: thus Shakespeare's *Works* or Milton's *Poems* would have no title entry under *Works* or under *Poems*, since these would be no help whatever to a person who did not have the author's name too. Title entries are also frequently omitted when the title begins with certain common words, such as *History, Introduction, Studies, Bibliography, Handbook, Manual,* and so on, because in many libraries the file of entries under one of these commonly used beginning words would grow quite bulky, and therefore difficult to use. While this rationale for omitting such entries is admittedly shaky (surely it is easier to find a title entry even in a very long file than to find one that isn't there at all), the practice of omitting them is almost universal in American libraries, and you should be aware of it. Otherwise, you may conclude that failure to discover a particular title entry means the book is not in the library, when in fact it is: what isn't in the library is the title entry. If both author and title approach fail to yield anything, you can always try looking for the book in the subject catalog, if you know what the subject is. Even if you fail to find the particular book you are seeking, you may find some other book in the subject catalog that will do just as well.

5. Entries with an umlauted vowel: An umlauted vowel is one which has suffered a sound change. In German the vowel A is normally pronounced as in "father"; but if the A is umlauted, as in "Händel," the sound approximates that of the A in "fate." The vowel has changed its sound. The Germans sometimes indicate an umlaut with the dieresis mark, as in "Händel," but they may also indicate it by putting the letter e after the vowel whose sound has changed. Thus "Händel" may also be written "Haendel." Many libraries (including the Library of Congress) therefore file all umlaut vowels (ä, ö, ü) *as if* they were followed by the letter e, whether they are or not, in order to keep variant forms of the same word together.

Thus you would find Händel filed *before* Hafer, because the imaginary e in Händel comes before the f in Hafer. Other libraries, however, file all umlauts exactly as spelled, and would thus file Händel *after* Hafer. When searching for an entry with an umlaut, always look for it in both possible positions, if you fail to find it where you looked first.

## THE SUBJECT CATALOG: FURTHER NOTES ON FILING[1]

In the subject catalog, an effort is made to group entries both logically and alphabetically, with results that may seem rather peculiar (and troublesome) to you, because alphabetical and logical arrangement are antithetical to each other. Listed below are two possible filing arrangements of the same subject headings. The column on the left is in the order followed in many subject catalogs, and, as you can see, it is not strictly alphabetical: the various divisions of the heading "Art" have been grouped in logical rather than alphabetical patterns. The column on the right is in word-by-word alphabetical order, which leads to an illogical sequence of headings.

| | |
|---|---|
| Art | Art |
| Art—Addresses, essays, lectures | Art, Abstract |
| Art—Africa | Art—Addresses, essays, lectures |
| Art—Bibliography | Art—Africa |
| Art—Catalogs | Art, Ancient |
| Art—Philosophy | Art and literature |
| Art—Rome (City) | Art and society |
| Art, Abstract | Art—Bibliography |
| Art, Ancient | Art, Byzantine |
| Art, Byzantine | Art—Catalogs |
| Art, Chinese | Art, Chinese |
| Art, Modern | Art dealers |
| Art, Primitive | Art, Modern |
| Art, Roman | Art objects |
| Art and literature | Art—Philosophy |
| Art and society | Art, Primitive |
| Art dealers | Art, Roman |
| Art objects | Art—Rome (City) |

Note carefully the sequence of headings in the left-hand column. First there is the main heading "Art," and then its subdivisions following the long dash. After all the subdivisions come the inverted adjectival forms,

[1] We will be talking here about filing subject entries in a divided catalog, where all subject entries are filed together in the subject section. The complexities and varieties of interfiling subject entries with author and title entries in a *dictionary* catalog (that is, an undivided catalog) are such that it would be pointless to go into them here. If your library has a dictionary catalog, and you want to know how subject entries are interfiled in it, then ask your librarian for a copy of the local filing rules and try to figure them out for yourself. You probably won't be able to, but at least you will understand better why the divided catalog is becoming increasingly popular.

and last of all the phrase headings "Art and literature," etc.

Since any subject catalog you work with may use either of the two basic patterns above, with any number of local variants, your first step in using the subject catalog should be to determine on what principle it has been filed. Otherwise you may waste your time looking for entries in the wrong place.

There is another departure from strict alphabetical arrangement which occurs in chronological subdivisions, used either as a direct subdivision of a main heading, or as a period division of the subdivision "History" and certain other subdivisions such as "Politics and government." An example of the first form follows:

English literature
English literature—Bibliography
English literature—Dictionaries
English literature—Study and teaching
English literature—Translations from Latin
English literature—Translations from Russian
English literature—Middle English (1100-1500)
English literature—Early modern (to 1700)
English literature—Early modern (to 1700)—History & criticism
English literature—18th century
English literature—19th century
English literature—19th century—Bibliography
English literature—19th century—History & criticism
English literature—20th century

The chronological subdivisions in this list are filed *after* all the form and topical subdivisions, the last of which is "Translations from Russian." The first chronological subdivision "Middle English (1100-1500)" files before all other chronological subdivisions because it comes chronologically (not alphabetically) before all the others. The last subdivision in the filing sequence is "20th century" because it comes last in point of time. To interfile chronological subdivisions alphabetically with other subdivisions would make them exceedingly difficult to find, especially if you did not know what particular name the cataloger had chosen for any particular time period. They would also be very difficult to find should you forget the principles of chronological arrangement that are usually followed in subject catalogs.

The second form of chronological subdivision is merely a more elaborate variant of the first, occurring after such subdivisions as "History." For example:

United States—History
United States—History—Addresses, essays, lectures
United States—History—Bibliography

United States—History—Dictionaries
United States—History—Fiction
United States—History—Pictorial works
United States—History—Sources
United States—History—Study and teaching
United States—History—Colonial period
United States—History—French and Indian War, 1755-1763
United States—History—Revolution
United States—History—Constitutional period, 1789-1809
United States—History—War with France, 1798-1800
United States—History—1801-1809
United States—History—Tripolitan War, 1801-1805
United States—History—1809-1817
United States—History—War of 1812
United States—History—1815-1861
United States—History—1817-1825
United States—History—1825-1829
United States—History—1849-1877
United States—History—Civil War
United States—History—20th century
United States—History—1919-1933
United States—History—1945-
United States—History, Local
United States—History, Military

When two chronological subdivisions begin with the same date, the more inclusive period files first: thus the subdivision "1801-1809" files before the subdivision "Tripolitan War, 1801-1805" because it covers a greater period of time, though it begins with the same date. After all the subdivisions of "United States—History" (both topical and chronological) you will find the inverted adjectival forms, beginning, in the list above, with "History, Local."

Since you are likely to forget (or never even know about) some of the rather complicated principles of filing, it is usually a good idea to look through a fairly wide range of relevant entries before giving up the search. This is a good rule of thumb to follow in using *any* kind of file, whether it be a catalog, a book index, a filing cabinet, or anything arranged in alphabetical order. In using the subject catalog, you should always determine first (when possible) from the Library of Congress list of subject headings that you have the correct subject-heading form for your topic, so that you will then have to contend only with the peculiarities of filing arrangement when you go to the catalog itself. If you still get negative results, you might then ask someone on the library staff for assistance. Failure to find what you are looking for in a subject catalog can seldom be regarded as conclusive, until you have called in expert assistance. Then if the results are still negative, you might ask your librarian to buy some books to fill up that lacuna in the collection.

# 8

# The Catalog:
# Corporate-Name Entries

The term "entry" in cataloging usage has two meanings: it is used (1) to denote a complete bibliographic citation for a given book, or (2) to denote the word or words by which a bibliographical citation is alphabetically filed in a catalog. In the first instance we might say a catalog has an entry for James Joyce's *Ulysses;* that is, a card has been filed in the catalog for some edition of this book. In the second instance, we might say that we have an author entry for James Joyce, meaning that there is a card in the catalog which is filed alphabetically by the name "Joyce, James." There would also be a title entry for this book; that is, a card would be filed alphabetically under the term *Ulysses.* The publisher of a book is not ordinarily used as an entry. In the case of Joyce's novel, for example, there would be no entry in the catalog for Shakespeare and Company, or Random House, or any of the other publishers of the book. But if someone should publish a book *about* the novel *Ulysses,* there would then be a subject entry for that book under the heading "Joyce, James—Ulysses."

In the second sense of the term, there are four general categories of entry in the catalog: personal-name entries, corporate-name entries, title entries, and subject entries (the last of which may embrace all three of the other kinds). We will discuss here only the corporate-name entry,[1] which is peculiarly troublesome to catalog users because of the unpredictability of the forms it may take. Suppose you were looking for some official publication of the Mexican Labor Department and looked for it under just that form of the department's name. You would find nothing in the catalog entered in that form and might conclude that there was therefore nothing

[1] Some twenty-five percent of main entries in library catalogs may be corporate-name entries.

issued by that department in the library. Your conclusion in this instance would be false or at least premature, because any publications the library owned by the Mexican Department of Labor would be entered thus: Mexico. Departamento del Trabajo. Names of government agencies are usually entered under the name of the country followed by the name of the agency *in the language of that country.* If you were looking for a publication by the Peace Corps or *about* the Peace Corps, you would find it entered thus: U. S. Peace Corps. A publication by or about the French Army would be entered: France. Armée.

Corporate-name entries are made not only for governments and their agencies, but also for various other corporate bodies, such as learned societies, institutions (museums, libraries, etc.), business firms, and conferences. Because it is usually very difficult (and sometimes impossible) to determine precisely what form of a corporate name has been chosen for a catalog entry, it is often easier to search for corporate publications under the editor's name (if there is an editor) or under the title of the publication, if you happen to know it, or even under a subject entry, if you are fairly certain what the subject is.

While it is impossible to list here even a fraction of the corporate-name forms that you are likely to encounter in a catalog, there are a few types which you may profitably keep in mind.

1. Names of governmental agencies are entered under the name of the country followed by the name of the agency in the language of the country:

> U.S. Army.
> Great Britain. Navy.
> France. Armée. Artillerie.
> Mexico. Ejército.

2. The laws of a nation, state, county, city, etc., are entered under the name of the political unit followed by the words "Laws, Statutes, etc.":

> U.S. Laws, Statutes, etc.
> North Carolina. Laws, Statutes, etc.
> Asheville. Laws, Statutes, etc.
> France. Laws, Statutes, etc.

3. The constitutions of various political units are entered under the name of the political unit followed by the word "Constitution." Thus, if you wanted to see a copy of the United States Constitution, you would look in the author-title catalog for the entry

> U.S. Constitution.

Or, if you wanted to find some books *about* the Constitution, you would then look in the subject catalog for the entry

U.S. Constitution.

4. Official publications of rulers are entered under the name of the political unit followed by the official name of the ruler's office:

U.S. President.
North Carolina. Governor.
Great Britain. Prime Minister.

Note: Most corporate-name forms may be used as subject headings in the subject catalog, but the rules for filing them can make them very difficult to find. For instance, the name of a government agency is *not* regarded as a topical subdivision of the country to which it belongs; it is therefore filed after *all* subdivisions of the country. Examples:

United States—Bibliography
United States—History, Military
United States—Territories and possessions
United States. Army
United States. Congress
United States. Congress. House.
United States. Congress, Senate. Committee on Commerce.
United States. Constitution.
United States. White Sands Proving Ground, N. M.
United States. Youth Conservation Corp.
United States Book Exchange

The last entry is for an organization that is not an official agency of the U.S. government; for that reason, it is not interfiled alphabetically with entries for organizations that are agencies of the government. Apples are kept on shelves separate from oranges as a matter of convenience, but this division is not much help when you don't know in the first place whether it is an apple or an orange that you are looking for. If you should mistakenly imagine that the United States Book Exchange is a government agency, you would expect to find it filed between "U.S. Army" and "U.S. Congress," and you would be wrong. By now you may have begun to suspect that the chief function of a cataloger is to make and arrange entries in such a way that ordinary mortals can never find them in a catalog. It is not easy to allay this suspicion, but it will help if you try to imagine some simpler way of constructing a catalog than the one you know. You will probably find that each new simplification generates some fresh complexity, and then you will begin to appreciate the cataloger's predicament and learn to make the most of his solution.

The purpose of this introduction to corporate-name entries is not to make you proficient in their use, but simply to make you aware of their existence and of the difficulty of determining precisely what form they may take. Whenever you are looking for a publication which you think was issued by some corporate body, it is usually a good idea to ask a librarian for help when you find that you cannot locate it by yourself. The important thing here is to be aware of a potential need for help whenever you begin to search the author-title or subject catalog for a corporate-name entry.

# 9

# Government Documents

Of the thousands of ancient writings that have come down to us on clay tablets and stone, the great bulk prove to be neither poetry, drama, fiction, nor sacred texts. They are instead those most indispensable instruments for the smooth functioning of an advanced civilization—government documents. Laws, tax rolls, annals of government, decrees, proclamations, the myriad records of obligations and rights that link a people and their government together—all these things were as familiar to educated Mesopotamians of 2000 B.C. as they are to us today. No less than the arts of agriculture and administration, government documents have always figured prominently in the development of civilization.

Their numerical preponderance, in relation to all other kinds of writing, testifies amply to their significance as a class of literature, even if the style and content of individual specimens sometimes belie the worth of the genre. Some 18,000 new document titles are recorded annually in the *Monthly Catalog of United States Government Publications,* an output approaching the aggregate production of the nation's commercial publishers. And the listing in the *Monthly Catalog,* vast though it is, only skims the surface. How much lies below, no one knows. For the making of a bibliographical net large enough to dip below the surface has never been attempted, so great would be the task. (Some hundred thousand research reports alone are published each year by the government, most of them never listed in the *Monthly Catalog.)*

Government documents are as various in their content as they are vast in their numbers. Ranging in price from nothing to a hundred dollars (the average price of the 78,000,000 publications sold each year by the Government Printing Office is 35 cents), and in size from a pamphlet of two pages to the elephantine *Subject Headings Used in the Dictionary Catalogs of the Library of Congress,* documents touch all areas of human interest. Everything is there—from a recipe for cooking dry beans to reports on the blast effects of nuclear weapons. Should you wish to brush up on your Burmese, read a lecture on poetic metaphor, design a cow barn, pave a runway in Antarctica, learn more about environmental pollution or congressional action on women's rights, there is a government document to help you. Often it is the best help available. When Matthew Josephson sought reliable first-hand information about the American monopolists whose tangled enterprises fill the pages of *The Robber Barons,* he got little help from their authorized biographies, which were mostly paid-for praise, or from their scanty personal papers. Much of the substance of the book came rather from government documents: lengthy verbatim transcripts of congressional hearings where the barons of steel, railroads, and oil were compelled to disclose the elaborate mysteries of their moneymaking exploits. Tracing the stream of historical, economic, and sociological writing back to its source, we commonly find a deep pool of government documents at the headwaters.

The nature and scale of popular interest in documents are exemplified by the twelve all-time best sellers of the Government Printing Office's 27,000 in-print titles:

| Title | Number Sold |
|---|---|
| Infant Care | 14,969,887 |
| Your Federal Income Tax | 14,194,594 |
| Prenatal Care | 9,224,878 |
| Your Child From 1 to 6 | 6,697,267 |
| Tax Guide for Small Business | 3,360,376 |
| Your Child from 6 to 12 | 3,230,192 |
| Your Social Security | 2,180,474 |
| Marihuana: Some Questions and Answers | 2,147,600 |
| LSD: Some Questions and Answers | 2,003,700 |
| Rescue Breathing | 1,984,800 |
| Narcotics: Some Questions and Answers | 1,908,200 |
| Syphilis & Gonorrhea | 1,906,838 |

How does one go about obtaining a government document? The principal means are these: buy it from a government bookstore (there were fifteen in 1972), order it from the Government Printing Office in Washington, order it from the government agency that issued it, ask your congressman if he can send you a free copy, or try to locate a copy in your library.

Libraries with the largest collections of documents are "depository libraries," so called because the government deposits in them at no cost any of a vast range of new documents as they come off the presses. "Regional depository libraries," of which there are some 36, must accept and house permanently everything offered to them by the Superintendent of Documents. The latest revision (1962) of the law regulating depository libraries provides for two in each congressional district and two more in each state. Together with depositories in the executive departments and agencies, the maximum authorized is about 1,350. Academic libraries account for more than half the total. The list of depository libraries printed in each September issue of the *Monthly Catalog* is a convenient guide to libraries in your area that maintain substantial documents collections. Non-depository libraries may build significant collections also, but are more selective in their acquisitions since most of their documents must be paid for.

Whether you have access to a depository library or not, the problem of identifying and locating specific documents is much the same, although in a depository you are more likely to have at hand the help of a specialist to guide you through the maze. Given the enormous scope and variety of government publications, the bibliographical apparatus created to identify them is, as you might suppose, vast, complex, and unwieldy. Three general guides are available. All are indispensable for those who work extensively with documents:

Schmeckebier, Laurence F., and Eastin, Roy B. *Government Publications and Their Use.* 2nd rev. ed. Washington, D. C.: Brookings Institution, 1969.

Boyd, Anne M. *United States Government Publications.* 3rd ed. rev. by Rae Elizabeth Rips. N. Y.: H. W. Wilson, 1949.

Childs, James B. *Government Document Bibliography in the United States and Elsewhere.* Washington, D. C.: Government Printing Office, 1942.

An excellent guide to bibliographies of government publications is Alexander C. Body's *Annotated Bibliography of Bibliographies on Selected Government Publications.* . . . . ([Kalamazoo]: Western Michigan University, 1967), a work periodically updated with supplements. Of the multitudinous bibliographies themselves, the major ones are these, covering the period indicated:

| | |
|---|---|
| 1774-1881 | Poore, Benjamin Perley. *A Descriptive Catalogue of the Government Publications of the United States.* . . .Washington, D.C.: Government Printing Office, 1885. |
| 1881-1893 | Ames, John Griffith. *Comprehensive Index to the Publications of the United States Government,* 1881-1893. 2 vols. Washington: GPO, 1905. |
| 1893-1940 | U. S. Superintendent of Documents. *Catalog of the Public Documents of Congress and All Departments of the Government of the United States.* . . .25 vols. Washington: GPO, 1896-1945. |
| 1895 to date | _____. *Monthly Catalog of United States Government Publications.* Washington: GPO, 1895- |

The last is the principal device for identifying current documents. Although far from comprehensive, as noted above, it is vast in scope and often the first and easiest point of approach. Entries are grouped in each issue alphabetically by the issuing department or bureau. A table of contents and an index (author, subject, title) are provided in each issue, and a cumulative annual index is printed in each December issue. (There are also decennial indexes to facilitate retrospective searches.) The index for 1971 contains about 50,000 entries covering 18,219 documents, giving three access points (average) for each item listed. Documents are given serial number identification, the first listed each year being 1, rising in serial order to the last (18,219 in 1971). Index entries cite the serial number for quick location of document citations within the main body of the catalog.

Prefatory matter in each issue of the *Monthly Catalog* describes concisely its organization and content, and will not be repeated here. But a word about the classification of government documents, and the practices of libraries in cataloging them is in order.

Many libraries make no entries in their card catalogs for most government documents. The larger the document collection the library owns, the more likely this is to be the case. After what has been said above about the significance of these publications, you may well wonder why libraries exclude them from their catalogs. It is mainly a matter of numbers. The cost of cataloging large document collections would overwhelm any library's budget. To avoid an expense that could not be borne anyhow, a library may use the *Monthly Catalog* itself as its own catalog of holdings, placing a penciled checkmark in the margin beside each item the library owns. So far so good—assuming you are aware that failure to find a document entry in the card catalog is inconclusive, since usually none is there even for documents the library owns. But if you find a checkmarked entry in the *Monthly Catalog,* how will you know where it is shelved in the library without a call number? The answer is that a call number is provided in the *Monthly Catalog* itself, at the lower-right corner of each citation. Based on neither LC nor Dewey classification, it is called a Superintendent of Documents classification number, and is used by libraries as a call number *for all documents not entered in the card catalogs* of the library. (A library-cataloged document may bear either a SuDocs number, or the usual LC or Dewey number.) As you may imagine, a library that arranges documents by the SuDocs numbers will shelve documents as a collection separate from all others, to keep the sequence of call numbers coherent. The effect of SuDocs classification is, mainly, to bring together on the shelves all publications of a given department, bureau, congressional committee, etc. Like all library classification schemes, it is grossly imperfect, since two publications issued by two different departments on the same subject will be widely separated from each other on the shelves. But as a shelf-location device it works well enough, and spares the library the enormous expense of using some other classification scheme. If your library maintains a separate document collection, a copy of the Superintendent of Documents classification outline will be available to guide you in using it.

Even in libraries that maintain extensive document collections, certain documents—mainly those that in scope and content appear indistinguishable from commercially published books—will be cataloged, classified, and shelved with the general book collection. This practice causes little or no difficulty for anyone. But failure to realize that the bulk of documents may be neither recorded in the card catalog nor shelved with the general collection may cause you to pass over inadvertently some of the most valuable materials on your subject. When in doubt, ask the reference librarian if there is a separate document collection. If there is, there is likely to be a specialist on the staff to help you use it. Ask.

More selective than the *Monthly Catalog,* and thus handier for spotting items of general interest, is the Superintendent of Documents' *Selected U. S. Government Publications.* Issued twice each month (free on request), this booklet lists general publications and maps of interest to the layman, including annotations where needed. The *Public Affairs Information Service Bulletin* (commonly called *PAIS),* a general index to all types of books, pamphlets, journal articles, etc. dealing with government and related topics, also indexes government documents, going beyond the *Monthly Catalog* to include state and local documents as well as federal (to which the *Monthly Catalog* is confined). *PAIS* is especially valuable for its complete citations to congressional hearings on issues of current interest. When searching for materials on economics, sociology, government, and legislation in *PAIS,* you will be automatically reminded by the index itself that documents comprise a substantial part of the literature of your subject. If for no other reason, *PAIS* should be routinely consulted during searches into these fields.

Bibliographical access to state documents is usually a difficult business. The most comprehensive listing is the *Monthly Checklist of State Publications,* issued by the Library of Congress but covering only those documents received by the Library. Some states issue lists of their own publications, giving better coverage than the *Monthly Checklist;* but often there are gaps and indexes are rare. The bibliography of local government publications is even spottier. *PAIS* covers some of these; but if *PAIS* and the *Monthly Checklist* let you down, you can keep the quest alive by writing or visiting the state or municipal library that is likely to collect the documents.

Like other publications, documents may receive attention in the review journals. Those of profound public interest, like the Warren Commission's report on the assassination of President Kennedy, or the Moynihan report on the Negro family, may provoke extensive review treatment, followed by a flurry of book-length analysis, criticism, and rebuttal by private authors. Among the journals that list or review documents are *American Political Science Review, Journal of Marketing, Wall Street Journal, American City, Law Library Journal,* and *Library Journal.*

Many documents are published as periodicals. An appendix to the February, 1972 *Monthly Catalog* lists more than 1,200 such titles. Many of these are regularly indexed in *Readers' Guide, Social Sciences & Humanities Index, Education Index, PAIS,* and other commercial indexes. The following titles convey some idea of the scope of government periodicals:

> *Economic Indicators*
> *Monthly Labor Review*
> *Survey of Current Business*
> *Wholesale Price Index*
> *Federal Reserve Bulletin*
> *American Education*
> *Department of State Bulletin*
> *Public Health Reports*
> *Social Security Bulletin*
> *Retail Food Price Index*
> *Water Resources Review*

A very complete guide to these publications is

Andriot, John L. *Guide to U. S. Government Serials and Periodicals.* 2 vols. McLean, Va.: Documents Index, 1972.

Nothing has been said thus far about the documents of other nations. They have them too, in such abundance that even a superficial survey would require more space than is available for this whole book. Suffice it to say that the bibliographical problems are much the same as those presented by American documents, with the difficulties of foreign languages superadded.

United Nations documents are a rich source of economic, political, and sociological data for the whole family of nations. The chief index is the *United Nations Documents Index,* begun in 1950 and issued monthly. A useful guide is Brimmer's *A Guide to the Use of United Nations Documents* (Dobbs Ferry, N.Y.: Oceana Pubs., 1962). UN publications deserving special mention are its *Demographic Yearbook,* a principal source of world population, migration, and sociological data; its *Statistical Yearbook,* also worldwide in coverage; and its *Yearbook,* covering issues and decisions of the organization during the year. The numerous publications of the United Nations Educational, Scientific and Cultural Organization (UNESCO) contain a wealth of current, authoritative information on the world at large.

To return to documents of the U. S. Government: Of the millions in existence, there are a select few of such transcendent importance to all citizens concerned, as Thomas Jefferson thought they ought to be, with the workings of their government and the conduct of their elected representatives, that a survey of them here, with brief comment, seems warranted. That way you will be sure of knowing at least the most basic steps to discovering just how well or badly you are being served by the men and women you elected with your votes, and paid with your taxes, to serve you. The price of freedom, it has been said, is eternal vigilance. Some of that vigilance has to do with mastering the basic bibliography of government publications.

## GOVERNMENT ORGANIZATION

The basic work is the *United States Government Organization Manual.* Begun in 1935 and published annually, this is the official handbook of the Federal Government. In the Foreword (1971/72) we are told that "it contains descriptions of the agencies of the legislative, judicial, and executive branches," plus a new section, "Sources of Information," which "gives helpful information to those interested in employment, contracting with the Federal Government, environmental programs, small business opportunities, publications, speakers and films available to civic and educational groups, as well as programs and activities of specific agencies." Mailing addresses and rosters of congressmen and appointed officers are included, together with detailed summary statements of the creation, authority, and duties of each unit of government. The text begins with the Constitution of the United States, from which all else flows, and the volume concludes with indexes of names and subjects that run about a hundred pages. Here is the whole government writ small.

For a larger view of congressional organization, there is the *Official Congressional Directory,* first published in 1809. Including biographical entries (of *Who's Who* length) for all congressmen and principal officers of the executive and judicial branches, it also gives rosters of congressional committees cross-indexed by members' names (a convenient device for determining what committees who serves on). There is also a roster of journalists formally admitted to the "Press Galleries" (including special designation of those whose wives or husbands, or whose "unmarried daughters in society" may accompany them); maps of all congressional districts; and a plethora of miscellaneous information relating to Congress and other branches of government. The volume concludes with an index of personal names currently running to more than a hundred pages, but no index of subjects at all.

Similar in content, but more elaborate and (usually) more current in its data, is the *Congressional Staff Directory,* which confines itself wholly to information about the Congress.

## FEDERAL LAWS

The entire Code (laws) of Hammurabi, inscribed on a stele of black diorite ca. 2200 B.C., contained 8,000 words spread over 49 columns. Schmeckebier and Eastin (cited above) use 18,000 words spread over 50 pages just to give a concise bibliographical outline of the laws of the United States.

The two major compilations of federal law are the *Statutes at Large,* an ongoing cumulation of the laws as they are enacted, and the *United States Code,* a compilation of general and permanent laws currently in force. The latest edition is 1970; cumulative supplements are issued after each session of Congress. Index entries refer to title and section number, and a separate index enters acts by their popular names.

Various separate indexes to the *Statutes at Large* and the *U. S. Code* have been compiled at various times, the most comprehensive being McClenon and Gilbert's *Index to the Federal Statutes 1874-1931,* a work of 1,432 pages that would have strained the stone supply of Babylon had Hammurabi been equally prolific of legislation.

Besides the two major compilations, most government offices having contact with the public also issue compilations of statutes relating to their own powers. Among these are laws relating to agriculture, atomic energy, banking and currency, copyright, foreign relations, government administration, Indian affairs, the military establishment, taxation, war, and water resources.

Of particular interest to citizens who wonder how their taxes are spent are the annual volumes of *Appropriations, Budget Estimates, etc.* and *The Budget of the United States Government.* Our English word "idiot" derives from a Greek term meaning "he who takes no interest in the affairs of his government." It is aptly applied to any citizen who does not know, and will not trouble himself to find out, how his government spends his money.

## CONGRESS

What *are* your 535 elected representatives and senators up to? What did they say on the floor of Congress, and how did they vote? What legislation was acted on, and how did it fare? The principal source of such information is the *Congressional Record,* begun in 1873 and continuing the record of the three earlier commercially published series: *Annals of Congress* (1789-1824), *Register of Debates* (1824-37), and *Congressional Globe* (1833-73).

Printed and issued daily (unbound), and with biweekly cumulations (paperbound) and permanent bound volumes that appear a year or more after the others, the *Record* is and always was something more and less than a verbatim account of what was actually said on the floor. More because each of its 535 editors (the congressmen themselves) may add whatever they please to its contents (anything from a snatch of favorite doggerel, to a speech the congressman never gave, to the 504-page list of World War I draft dodgers appended in 1921 at the request of a congressman); less because each editor may also delete or revise remarks he made on the floor "in the ardor of discussion" and thus keep indecorous, insulting, or erroneous statements from entering the *Record*. (The *Record* leaves no record of the torrid conflict in which Senator Morse referred to Senator Capehart as "a cup of rancid ignorance.") Unlike the rest of us, congressmen in the aftermath of warm debate may say "I wish I'd said that," and then make it appear they actually did. The permanently bound volumes of the *Record* undergo a second editorial revision, and are thus not identical either in content or page numbering to the daily and biweekly issues.

In any case the *Congressional Record* is as close as we will ever come to knowing what happened on the floors of Congress, and the reports of business transacted may be regarded as faithful accounts of real events. Indexes are issued biweekly (non-cumulative) and a cumulative index is compiled for the bound volumes at the end of each session. Subject entries are weak, but entries by members' names and bill numbers are strong. To trace debate on a given subject, it is therefore generally necessary to identify (in the index by bill numbers) the number of the bill under debate, and proceed from there.

An excellent device for tracing the progress of bills through the maze of committee hearings, floor debates, amendments, conference committees, etc., is the looseleaf *Congressional Index*, published and kept current through the year by the Commerce Clearing House, Inc. This valuable service also provides complete voting records on all bills — the most tangible evidence possible on how your congressmen actually stood on issues that concern you.

## CONGRESSIONAL COMMITTEE HEARINGS

These documents are indispensable not only for finding out what is going on in the legislative councils, but also for finding out what is going on in the nation and in the world at large. Under the power of subpoena, committees may summon to hearings any citizen whose personal knowledge is thought to bear on the business at hand—which is usually the development of legislation that may, and often does, vitally affect the personal welfare of the citizenry, and the security of the nation. The following list of some committee hearings published over the last decade suggests the range and import of these documents:

| | |
|---|---|
| Population Crisis | Federal Highway Acts |
| Drug Safety | Role of Giant Corporations |
| Public Television | Tax-Exempt Foundations |

| | |
|---|---|
| National Parks | Housing & Urban Development |
| Economic Concentration | Discrimination Against Women |
| Failing Newspaper Act | Mass Transportation |
| Wiretapping | Civil Rights |
| Selective Service System | Crime in America |
| Voting Rights | Water Pollution |
| Alcoholism | Military Budget |
| Coal Mine Health & Safety | Campus Unrest |
| National Health Insurance | Equal Educational Opportunity |
| Migratory Labor Legislation | Juvenile Delinquency |
| Examination of the War on Poverty | Tax Reform |
| Nutrition and Human Needs | Failing Railroads |
| Air Pollution | |

Committee hearings are not the dry-as-dust documents you may imagine. Under the direction of an aggressive chairman, supported by the meticulous researches of an able staff, these hearings regularly elicit testimony of vital consequence in diagnosing the failings of our national life and finding remedies for them. Testimony and questioning are sometimes pungent and dramatic, always informative. An excerpt from Ralph Nader's concluding testimony on dangerous automobile designs in the hearings entitled *Federal Role in Traffic Safety* (March 22, 1966) illustrates some of the fascination of these hearings:

*Senator Kennedy.*   Now I would like to ask you perhaps just one final question. Why are you doing all of this, Mr. Nader?

*Mr. Nader.* . . . If I was engaged in activities for the prevention of cruelty [to] animals, nobody would ever ask me that question. Because I happen to have a scale of my priorities which leads me to engage in activities for the prevention of cruelty to humans, my motivations are constantly inquired into.

Basically the motivation is simply this. When I see, as I have seen, people decapitated, crushed, bloodied, and broken, and that is what we are really talking about in auto safety, when we get down to it it is the fatalities and the horrible carnage involved, when I see that on highways, as I have seen all over the country, going back many years, I ask myself what can the genius of man do to avoid it? . . .

Now in this country we have decided that while we may send people to jail for fixing prices, we don't send people to jail for designing defective automobiles. If that is going to be the assumption, and I think it should be questioned, if that is going to be the assumption, all the more do we need safeguards on corporation behavior in terms of preventative action, standards by government, and so forth, to improve the quality of product that comes out.

Earlier in the day, before the same subcommittee, President Roche of General Motors made his celebrated public apology to Ralph Nader for the unwarranted surveillance of his private life initiated by General Motors in retaliation for his criticisms of their automobiles. The dramatic flavor of the close and persistent questioning of witnesses that is a characteristic feature of committee hearings is well captured in one episode that followed President Roche's apology:

*Senator Ribicoff.* Spell your name.

*Mr. Bridenstine.* B-r-i-d-e-n-s-t-i-n-e. I am Mr. Power's assistant, assistant general counsel [of General Motors].

*Senator Kennedy.* First let me ask you do you agree with Mr. Roche's statement and apologies to Mr. Nader?

*Mr. Bridenstine.* Wholeheartedly, Senator.

*Senator Kennedy.* Do you agree with it?

*Mr. Bridenstine.* Wholeheartedly.

*Senator Kennedy.* And apologies in connection with it?

*Mr. Bridenstine.* Apologies to this committee, to the Senate, to Mr. Nader.

*Senator Kennedy.* Let me ask you then when the statement of March 9 [issued by General Motors] was being drawn up, were you aware of the fact that the investigation had gone beyond the question of routine investigation?

*Mr. Bridenstine.* I knew only what was in the report, in looking at the copies that had come in.

*Senator Kennedy.* That indicated, did it not, that there had been a surveillance?

*Mr. Bridenstine.* I knew that there was a surveillance because there was an indication that there had been a surveillance; yes, sir.

*Senator Kennedy.* If you could just answer the question. You are both lawyers. Just say yes or no.

*Mr. Bridenstine.* Yes.

*Senator Kennedy.* You knew it?

*Mr. Bridenstine.* Yes, I knew it.

*Senator Kennedy.* And then did you know that they had inquired into Mr. Nader's sex life?

*Mr. Bridenstine.* No; I did not.

*Senator Kennedy.* Did you know that, sir?

*Mr. Power.* No.

*Senator Kennedy.* Did you read the reports?

*Mr. Bridenstine.* Yes, sir.

*Senator Kennedy.* But you didn't see anything about that?

*Mr. Bridenstine.* I didn't know anything about the questions. I read the report. I still don't know what they asked

*Senator Kennedy.* Let me rephrase it. Do you know there had been things in the report regarding Mr. Nader's sex life?

*Mr. Bridenstine.* The only thing I read in the report was good about Mr. Nader.

*Senator Kennedy.* Now, now, now, now, I am not questioning that Mr. Nader's sex life wasn't good. [Laughter.]

At the end of this relentless questioning, the quarry is trapped. Mr. Bridenstine is sharply rebuked by Senator Kennedy for his deceptiveness, and partly as a result of all this Mr. Nader collected substantial damages from General Motors, enabling him thereafter to expand his exposés of corporate America.

It is no rare thing to come on high drama in congressional committee hearings, for it is here that the most serious concerns of the nation are periodically aired. What is rare is to find a citizen who knows anything about this major branch of our national literature.

Prior to 1924 printings of hearings were limited, intended chiefly for the use of the committee. Following criticism of this practice by scholars and librarians, press runs were enlarged and access made easier through placement of orders with the Superintendent of Documents. In 1938 a law was passed enabling depository libraries to receive all hearings as printed. Some hearings are never printed and many others soon go out of print, especially those on controversial current issues, and can only be obtained in libraries that acquired them shortly after publication.

Hearings are commonly referred to by the name of the committee or subcommittee that held them. There is little uniformity in the titling and numbering of them, but the subject index of the *Monthly Catalog* gives fairly reliable access. Hearings are grouped under committee name in the Congress section of the main body of the *Monthly Catalog*. There is often a lapse of two to six months between a hearing date and the listing in the *Monthly Catalog*—by which time the entire printing may well be sold out.

Besides a full verbatim transcript of testimony, hearings usually print substantial supporting materials from various printed sources—books, periodicals, newspapers—plus excellent bibliographies of the topic at hand. Their value as source material on great national issues cannot be overstated.

## PRESIDENTIAL PAPERS

There are many sources for the messages and papers of the presidents. Messages are always published in the *Congressional Record* and are easily located through the index. An important collection is

Richardson, James D. *A Compilation of the Messages and Papers of the Presidents, 1789-1897.* . . . 20 vols. N. Y.: Bureau of National Literature [1917?].

Though not all-inclusive, it is a useful compilation, and its encyclopedic index is a great help to the researcher. In 1958 publication was begun on a major series entitled *Public Papers of the Presidents of the United States,* issued by the Federal Register Division of the National Archives. Papers of the following have appeared to date: Harry S. Truman (8 vols.), Dwight D. Eisenhower (8 vols.), John F. Kennedy (3 vols.), and Lyndon B. Johnson (10 vols.).

An official source for presidential proclamations, executive orders, and other presidential documents is the *Federal Register* (1936- ), a serial usually available only in large libraries. Recent presidential messages are readily found in the *Department of State Bulletin,* the *New York Times,* and *A Weekly Compilation of Presidential Documents* (issued by the Office of the Federal Register). The latter includes public speeches, messages to Congress, remarks, and transcripts of presidential news conferences, and is well indexed.

## STATISTICS

The Federal Government is the nation's chief gatherer and disseminator of statistical data. A summary of its harvest is published annually as the *Statistical Abstract of the United States,* which also includes an extensive guide to other sources of statistical data. Some companion volumes are

> *Congressional District Data*
> *County & City Data Book*
> *Historical Statistics of the United States*
> *Directory of Non-Federal Statistics for States and Local Areas*
> *Directory of Federal Statistics for States*
> *Directory of Federal Statistics for Local Areas*

Detailed information on all federal agencies and departments issuing statistical data is given in

U. S. Bureau of the Budget. *Statistical Services of the United States Government.* Rev. ed. Washington, 1968.

Another useful volume listing sources by subject is

Andriot, John L. *Guide to U. S. Government Statistics.* 3rd ed. Arlington, Va.: Documents Index, 1961.

Entries specify frequency of publication, availability and price, and SuDocs classification numbers.

A readable and handy volume dealing with statistical sources in the United States, the United Kingdom, and international organizations is Joan M. Harvey's *Sources of Statistics* (Hamden, Conn.: Archon Books, 1969). Each chapter is devoted to a single subject: population, social statistics, education, labor, production, trade, finance, prices, transport and communication, and tourism. Many of the publications cited are government documents.

## CENSUS PUBLICATIONS

By far the most prolific of all statistical producers, the U. S. Bureau of the Census issues a quarterly and an annual bibliography (with monthly supplements) of its own multitudinous publications, but has had trouble making up its mind what to call it. Variously titled *Census Publications, Catalog and Subject Guide* (1945-51), *Catalog of United States Census Publications* (1952-62), *Bureau of the Census Catalog of Publications* (1963), it has settled down since 1964 with the simple title *Bureau of the Census Catalog.* The bibliography of publications from the first census (1790) through 1945 is covered by:

U. S. Library of Congress. *Catalog of United States Census Publications, 1790-1945.* Washington: GPO, 1950.

The population census, taken every decade since 1790, is the oldest. Other major census topics are manufactures (since 1810), agriculture (1840), mining (1840), state and local governments (1850), retail, wholesale, and service trades (1929), housing (1940), foreign trade (1941), construction industry (1959), and transportation (1963). So voluminous are the full census reports that only the largest libraries can devote shelf space to house a substantial portion of them. Most libraries rely mainly on the current population census and digests such as *Statistical Abstracts* to keep their patrons abreast of the latest count.

## FOREIGN AFFAIRS

Documents in this field are generated principally by the Department of State and the Senate Committee on Foreign Relations. Treaties, the numerous spawn of successful foreign relations, create political order and bibliographical confusion. Irregular in numbering and designation, and published in a great variety of series, treaties are currently being assembled and placed in rational order by the State Department in an ongoing publication called *Treaties and Other International Agreements of the United States of America, 1776-1949,* which will run about 15 volumes when complete. An excellent bibliography of treaties currently in effect is *Treaties in Force: A List of Treaties and Other Agreements of the United States,* published annually by the State Department. Each entry also specifies where the published text of the treaty may be found (e.g., in *U. S. Statutes at Large, United Nations Treaty Series,* etc.). For very recent information on the status of treaties one turns to the *Department of State Bulletin,* issued weekly.

The basic set of official papers dealing with foreign relations is now known as *Foreign Relations of the United States—Diplomatic Papers,* after several title changes since the series began in 1861. Prior to that date these materials were contained in annual congressional documents. The set now runs to more than 250 volumes.

## DEPARTMENTAL REPORTS

Many report series of government agencies have outstanding research value in their varied fields. Some examples are

Geological Survey. *Annual Report.* 1880-
Indian Affairs Office. *Annual Report.* 1825-
American Ethnology Bureau. *Annual Report.* 1880-
————. *Bulletins.* 1886-
Smithsonian Institution. *Annual Report.* 1846-

## MAPS AND CHARTS

Systematic and extensive publication of maps in series commenced in the late nineteenth century. Navigation charts of foreign waters were produced for public use around 1837, and Coast and Geodetic Survey charts of coastal waters started publication in 1844. The Corps of Engineers produced the first charts of the Great Lakes in 1852. And four major geographical and geological surveys of the West were conducted late in the century. But there was no coordination of all this mapping activity, nor a systematic plan for mapping the whole country until 1879, when the U. S. Geological Survey took on the task and developed a master plan.

At present the Geological Survey supervises mapping through its three sections: Topographic Maps, Aerial Photography, and Geodetic Control. Generally speaking, maps may be purchased from the agencies' publishing them, and some are available from the Superintendent of Documents. Some notable mapmaking agencies are the Bureau of Land Management (maps of national parks, Indian reservations, reclamation projects, etc.), the Geological Survey, the Coast and Geodetic Survey, the Federal Power Commission (maps of generating stations, transmission lines, natural gas pipelines), the Bureau of Public Roads, the Weather Bureau, the Army, Navy, Air Force, and Corps of Engineers, the Civil Aeronautics Board, and the State Department (international boundaries). Most agencies that sell maps also issue index maps and catalogs.

The National Archives maintains the most complete collection of government-made maps, publishes lists and catalogs of them, and also sells photoreproductions of maps. The Library of Congress also maintains extensive map collections.

A recent and invaluable document in this area is *The National Atlas of the United States of America,* published in 1970 by the Geological Survey. An outstanding scholarly atlas bringing together and vividly depicting data from official primary sources, it contains general reference maps and special subject maps (physical, historical, economic, sociocultural, administrative, cartographical), covering such things as climate, soils, water resources, battle sites, agriculture, mineral and energy resources, manufacturing, business, population distribution, ethnic population, transportation, crime, natural gas pipelines, and family income distribution. There are also index maps and elaborate guides to mapping activities of the nation. Beautiful to behold and wonderfully stimulating to the intellect, this remarkable atlas is an indispensable research source for any inquiry into the life of the nation.

The field of government documents, as you must be thinking by now, is inexhaustible. The harvest is always plentiful no matter where or when you reap it. The great difficulty is in remembering that despite its vast expanse, this whole field of literature somehow remains invisible to most users of libraries, even when the materials are actually in the library.

To make matters worse, while great quantities of government documents are routinely distributed to libraries and are thus relatively easy of access, numerous reports, records, studies, statistical compilations, etc. of the various federal agencies are never issued for public distribution and, until the passage of the Public Information Act of 1966, were often withheld arbitrarily from citizens who knew of their existence, asked to see them, and were legally entitled to do so. The burden of proof was on the citizen to show that he was legally entitled to inspect documents denied to him by a federal agency. Under "the Freedom of Information Law," as the Act of 1966 is commonly called, the burden of proof is on the other side, and the agency must either release information upon request or prove that it is *not* legally bound to do so. This turnabout has naturally improved the flow of legally available government information to the citizenry.

The Act requires every federal agency to publish rules, regulations, and appeal procedures governing the release of its records. One need only consult the published rules to determine what information is legally available and what steps must be taken to obtain it. Fine so far. But these published rules are now scattered over more than a million printed pages— principally in the *Federal Register*—and for most people would therefore be as good as lost, except for the recent publication of a work that attempts to bring together all the pertinent data in two good-sized volumes:

Kerbec, Matthew J. (ed.). *Legally Available U. S. Government Information as a Result of the Public Information Act.* 2 vols. Arlington, Va.: Output Systems Corp., 1970.

Volume I (211 pages) treats the Department of Defense and NASA; volume II (536 pages) covers all other federal agencies.

Kerbec's compilation, and the Public Information Act that underlies it, are powerful tools for extracting material from the great treasury of information created by federal agencies, and sometimes withheld by them from the public until the public reminds them of their right to know.

# 10

# The Strategy of Search

If you have not already forgotten many of the titles of the indexes, bibliographies, encyclopedias, and other reference works that you have become acquainted with in the last eight chapters, you probably will forget most of them in a matter of weeks. This is unavoidable, memory being the frail thing that it is; but what you can and must remember is that such books do exist, and can be very useful to you if you also remember how to go about locating them when the need arises. This much remembrance is minimal.

By now you should also have developed some sense of strategy in the use of the library, for if you have not, you will hereafter be condemned to waste valuable time, which could be profitably spent in reading books rather than confusedly groping for them. If, for example, you require the date of some historical event, you would be foolish to spend time searching the subject catalog for a book which might yield that date, when you should be able to walk directly to the reference collection and find in a matter of moments some historical dictionary that would answer your needs. Or if you require the most current information on a given topic, it would be absurd to look for it in a *book* (where information is usually several years out of date on the day of publication) when there is no possibility of finding it anywhere except in recently published periodicals. The first step in any search problem should be reflection on the best strategy for solving it. To omit that step would be as foolish as starting out on a cross-country journey without consulting a road map.

In the outline below, a "model" strategy is presented which might be employed in whole or in part in the course of any research you might undertake in the writing of a term paper. Study it carefully, remembering that while it will be applicable to many search problems, there will be occasions when you will need to depart from it partially or entirely.

Assuming that you have only settled on the general subject area to be treated in your paper, the sequence of steps you would take in the library might be this:

1. Locate a book in the reference collection that gives a synopsis of your subject, so you can familiarize yourself with its more prominent features, learn something of its magnitude and historical development, and of the principal writers in the field, and thereby form some notion of what direction your own treatment of the subject might take. The problem of locating an appropriate reference book (if one is in the library) can be quickly resolved by determining from the classification outlines what *major* class your subject belongs to, and then going to the reference collection and, if necessary, briefly inspecting *every* reference book which the library owns in that class. If nothing suitable can be found in the major class, you can always turn to a general encyclopedia, and often you will want to do this in any case. Besides giving a synopsis of your subject, the reference books you consult may also give you a brief bibliography of the more important books in the field, one or more of which you may wish to examine before carrying your research any further. (Incidentally, by noting publication dates of books listed in a bibliography at the end of a reference article, you can usually tell approximately when the article itself was written—a matter of some importance, which can seldom be reliably determined from the date of publication of the reference book itself. The most recent edition of the *Encyclopaedia Britannica,* for example, contains numerous articles written in the nineteenth century, although the editors of the *Encyclopaedia* prefer to conceal this fact. But if a bibliography at the end of an article in the *Encyclopaedia* lists nothing but books published in the nineteenth century, you may be reasonably sure that the article itself was written not much later than the year 1900.).

2. After gaining some overview of your subject by reading about it in a reference book, your next step will be to determine where in the library you will find a *collection* of books dealing with the subject. This means that you will need to discover the specific classification range of your subject, either from the subject catalog or from the classification schedules. Then go to the shelves and make a general survey of the books that deal with your subject, and select for further reading those books which, after examination of their tables of contents and sampling of their style, appear to be most appropriate to your inquiry. (Whenever you examine *any* book, periodical article, or whatever, along the way, you should *always* make a complete and correct bibliography citation to it on a three-by-five note card, with appropriate comments as, for example, "Chapter 5 very important"; "Entertaining but superficial"; "Read whole book"; "Extensive bibliography at end"; "Good index"; and so on. In this way you will have at all times a complete chart of your researches, so nothing of value will be lost through forgetfulness. And when it comes time to make citations in the writing of your paper, you will already have your citations in correct form and will never find yourself in the awkward predicament of having to return to the shelves to check something in a book that someone else has charged out.)

3. Read the books you have selected, making careful notes on everything of potential value, and specifying the exact page in the book from which the note was taken. When making an exact transcription of a passage that runs on for more than one page, place a slash-mark at the point in the passage where one page ends and another begins; otherwise, if you choose to quote only a portion of the passage when you begin to write your paper, you will not be sure which page that *portion* appeared on. When in your reading you come upon references to other books that may be useful to you, make preliminary bibliography cards for them so you will remember later to examine those books also.

4. Develop a list of *specific* subject headings related to your topic, and then search the subject catalog to see if under these headings you can locate appropriate books which were *not* shelved with those in the specific class range (step 2, above). Examine these books and treat them as in steps 2 and 3, remembering that when you locate books in this fashion, you should always look at the other books shelved near them, because you may turn up something in this way even more suitable than what you had sought directly.

5. At this point you should be fairly well acquainted with your subject, and should be able to pinpoint the specific aspect of it which you will treat in your term paper. Now the digging begins.

6. With a list of the very specific facets of your subject which you wish to explore in depth, you may now begin to search for appropriate articles in periodicals, using the various general and specialized periodical indexes which you learned about in Chapter 3. Make formal citations (as you did with books) for everything you actually examine, and take notes on everything you read. In addition to periodical articles, you may also wish to consult other materials published in less-than-book-length form, and will find it essential to do so if you cannot find sufficient materials in book-length treatments of the subject and in periodical articles.

7. If you are working in a library whose collection is well developed in your subject field, you may now turn to a comprehensive published bibliography of your subject and see what additional materials you can discover in that way. (In a first-rate library, you might consult a published bibliography as the very next step after reading in the reference collection. But you could never afford to stop there, because a published bibliography will usually be a year, sometimes many years, out of date, so you will have to update it yourself by using your library's catalog as well as current periodical indexes.) In a library whose book collection is weak (and those of many college libraries are exceedingly so), a published bibliography can be extremely frustrating to use, because you will find listed in it so many titles which you would like to see, but cannot, because your library does not own them. Even so, a published bibliography can give you *some* help if you are patient enough to trace out the items listed in it which your library actually owns, or to search the holdings of other libraries.

8. At this point your systematic search for materials will be concluded, although as your reading and note-taking progress, you may continue to chase down specific items as the need for them arises. It will be helpful now to locate reviews of those books on which it appears you will draw most heavily in writing your paper, in order to obtain an expert appraisal of the value of your sources and to learn of other aspects of the subject which your author may have overlooked. Book reviewers for the most part are accomplished pickflaws, and are quick to call an author to task for his shortcomings. Reviewers of scholarly books often are (or imagine themselves to be) more knowledgeable than the authors themselves, and are never shy about making their superior wisdom available to you. This wisdom can be very helpful, if you will take the trouble to locate it. Authors have a knack for making their own point of view seem so plausible, even when it is fundamentally absurd, that its absurdity may escape you unless some authoritative critic points it out. The mere fact that a book has been published is no guarantee that all or any of its information is reliable. Motives of deception are not restricted to the spoken word.

You should now have a solid bibliographical foundation for supporting a structure of the dimensions of a term paper. If you suspect that you do not, then ask your instructor or a librarian to review what you have done and suggest other directions that your research might take. The sturdiness of your finished paper will be directly determined by the solidity of your bibliographical foundation: if you have built it carelessly, no amount of mere eloquence can prevent your paper from collapsing. But if you have built well, clear thinking and plain writing will guarantee a paper worthy of the time you have put into it and the time it will take your instructor to read it.

And you will make the very pleasant discovery that the task of writing a term paper becomes much less formidable when you are able to solve quickly the bibliographical problems that are inevitably associated with that task. Bibliography is the bedrock of all scholarship: once you have sunk your foundations securely into it, you can safely build to any height that your intelligence and imagination will lift you to.

# 11

# What is a Library?
# A Sceptical Postlude

We declare at the outset that we do not make any positive assertion that anything we shall say is wholly as we affirm it to be. We merely report accurately on each thing as our impressions of it are at the moment.

—Sextus Empiricus, *Outlines of Pyrrhonism*

Much has been said in the foregoing chapters about ways to use a library, but nothing was said about what a library is—as if that matter were too obvious for comment.

For everyone knows what a library is, or ought to be, until he begins to think deeply about it. Then perplexity arises.

It will not do to say that a library is simply a collection of books, since that definition will equally well cover a bookstore, a publisher's warehouse, or your parents' attic. Neither will it do to resort to platitude, and define a library as a repository of "the best that has been thought and known in the world," for a casual survey of the holdings of any library flatly refutes that notion. Take Hitler's *Mein Kampf,* for example—or yesterday's newspaper.

While it is difficult to get any general agreement as to what books—or even what *kinds* of books—ought to make up a library, librarians have been plagued for centuries by dogmatic persons who claim to know, at any rate, what a library ought *not* to be—that is, what particular books, or kinds of books, ought not be admitted to the library, or allowed to remain there if admitted by mistake. And library censors usually go beyond merely claiming to know what a library ought not to be. They take vigorous measures to see that, by removing certain books, or whole classes of books, the library is prevented from being what they feel it ought not to be.

Even in our own country, where political and intellectual freedom is constitutionally guaranteed, libraries are never immune to the onslaughts of the censor. By compulsion or choice, American librarians have at times banished from their collections the works of such authors as Mark Twain, William Faulkner, Pearl Buck, Henry Miller, J. D. Salinger, Karl Marx, and Edmund Wilson, to name only a few who aroused the censor's wrath. In 1885 the Public Library of Concord, Massachusetts banned *Huckleberry Finn* as "trash and suitable only for the slums." In 1941 Governor Talmadge ordered all Georgia college and school libraries to remove all books reflecting discredit upon the South, the Bible, or the state of Georgia. And in 1953 the state libraries of Illinois removed Sinclair Lewis's *Kingsblood Royal* along with six thousand other books "relating to sex" after a mother complained they had lent her daughter an offensive book.

Despite their public image of timidity, many librarians have stoutly resisted the repressive forces of censorship. Some have valiantly fought a losing battle right down to the last ditch, forfeiting their jobs and even their careers rather than submit to the censor's yoke. And others have submitted, either through fear for their livelihood, or the conviction that it is their duty to forbid access to offensive publications.

Alexander Solzhenitsyn in his novel *Cancer Ward*[1] depicts vividly the plight of the librarian caught in the censor's web:

"And what I'm telling you now—that's because they're ready to wheel me into the operating room. Even now I wouldn't dare utter it in the presence of a third person. I wouldn't! There. That's how far they've driven me to the wall. And I finished the agricultural academy, no less. I finished the advanced courses in historical and dialectical materialism. I lectured in several disciplines—and all this in Moscow! But then the great oaks began to topple. In the agricultural academy Professor Muralov was felled. They swept out professors by the dozen. Were we expected to confess errors? I confessed errors! Did we have to recant? I recanted! A certain percentage of us survived, didn't we? I was among these. I turned to pure biology; I thought I had found a safe, sheltered refuge. But the purge overtook even biology, and what a purge! The biology department faculties were swept clean. Give up lecturing? All right, I stopped, I became an assistant, I was willing to step down and become a nonentity."

The silent man of the ward, and how freely he talked! The words poured from him as though he were more accustomed to speaking than to anything else.

"The textbooks of great scientists were suppressed, the teaching programs were revised—all right, I went along with it, we'd teach in the new way. They told us to rewrite anatomy, microbiology and neuropathology according to the teachings of an ignorant agronomist and according to horticultural practices. Bravo, I agree, I'm in favor! No, that's not enough—give up your assistantship, too! All right, I won't argue, I'll become an instructor in agricultural methods. No, that wasn't enough of a sacrifice; they removed me from that job also. All right, I agree, I'll be a librarian, a librarian in remote Kokand! How far I had retreated! But nevertheless I was alive, and my children had been graduated from institutes.

[1] Alexander Solzhenitsyn, *Cancer Ward,* tr. Nicholas Bethell and David Burg (New York: Farrar, Straus and Giroux, 1969), pp. 506-508. Quoted by permission of the publisher.

They send librarians secret orders: Destroy the books on the pseudoscience of genetics! Destroy all books by such-and-such authors! Could I become inured to this? Well, hadn't I myself stood up in the dialectical materialism classroom a quarter of a century ago and denounced the theory of relativity as counterrevolutionary obscurantism? So I followed instructions and drew up the lists of books I had to burn, and the Party Organizer and the Special Division countersigned them, and we tossed them in the fire. Genetics! Leftist esthetics! Ethics! Cybernetics! Arithmetic! . . . "

He even laughed. The crazy raven!

". . . Why do we need bonfires in the streets and all that sort of superfluous dramatics? We did it in a quiet corner, we tossed the books into the furnace, the furnace gave heat. That's where they drove me, till I had my back to the furnace. But I managed to raise a family. My daughter, who edits the district paper, wrote this lyrical verse:

> *No, I shall never retreat.*
> *I don't know how to beg for pardon.*
> *If fight it's to be, our hearts*
> *'gainst even our fathers we'll harden."*

In American public schools and public libraries, the librarian himself usually turns out to be the most active and effective force of censorship.[2] Astonishing as it may seem, even in our college libraries—those supposed citadels of academic freedom—one sometimes finds plain evidence of the censor's hand at work, most commonly through the exclusion of sexually oriented works, like those of the Marquis de Sade and the Baron von Sacher-Masoch (whose names have become part of our standard vocabulary: "sadism" and "masochism"); or through the refusal to subscribe to any of the alternative press journals, or other magazines, like the *Evergreen Review* and *Ramparts,* that blatantly challenge the mores and politics of the American middle class. Wherever such publications are conspicuously absent from a library's collections, you may safely conclude the censor has done his job, denying you access to things you have a right to read by imposing his own definition of what a library ought not to be.

The problem of censorship may partly arise from a gross misconception of what a library is, or ought to be. If one of us should be asked point blank for a metaphor to describe a library, he would probably reply that it is a "temple of learning," "a storehouse of knowledge," "a treasury of wisdom," or something equally grand. Luminous and inspiring phrases, but using them uncritically causes needless mischief, for they lead people to expect something radically different from what actually fills the shelves of a library. These figures of speech hide reality behind a bogus ideal. They intimidate ordinary mortals with the suggestion that librarians

---

[2] Marjorie Fiske, *Book Selection and Censorship* . . . (Berkeley: Univ. of California Press, 1959), p. 123.

pile up only dry bones for their edification. And idealists are outraged when they discover the earthy portion of our libraries has been gilded with shining metaphors.

Fear and hatred of the written word—and by extension books and libraries—are passions from which philosophers, professors, and librarians are not wholly immune. An illiterate person is likely to feel awe and reverence for the art of writing, the making of books, and the building of libraries. But teach him to read and write and, behold, we have no longer a guaranteed reverencer of libraries, but a potential patron and a possible enemy of that art from which the profession of librarianship sprang. Marshall McLuhan is merely a recent example of the learned man who despises books; the phenomenon itself is ancient. It can be traced bibliographically to the fourth century B.C., and mythologically all the way back to the origin of writing.

Advocates of intellectual freedom will better appreciate the difficulty of their position when they consider that the greatest intellect of the Western world was himself openly hostile to it. Plato, in the *Phaedrus,* places in the mouth of Socrates an argument contrived to discredit whatever virtue the written word may appear to possess. Socrates tells how the god Ammon spoke scornfully to Thoth, the mythical inventor of writing, when he boasted that his invention was "an elixir of memory and wisdom." If the Egyptians learn to write, says Ammon,

> Their trust in writing will discourage the use of their own memory within them. You have invented an elixir not of memory, but of reminding; and you offer your pupils the appearance of wisdom, not true wisdom, for they will read many things, when they are for the most part ignorant and hard to get along with, since they are not wise, but only appear wise.

Expounding upon the myth, Socrates concludes that written words are useless "except to remind him who knows the matter about which they are written." The proper mode of instruction is therefore dialogue between student and teacher, since books are useful for learning only what one already knows. And the written word suffers the further disadvantage—which dialogue escapes—of being "bandied about, alike among those who understand and those who have no interest in it, and it knows not to whom to speak or not to speak; when ill-treated or unjustly reviled it always needs its father to help it, for it has no power to protect or help itself." The argument against writing, placed in the context of Plato's other dialogues, attests to his fear that the book might offer enlightenment to the masses (for whom he had no use), and expose to attack his own notions of the true and the good when he would no longer be around to defend them. And yet, through a peculiar impulse common to enemies of the book, Plato commits to writing his fear of writing, thus equipping us to do what he wished to prevent.

Intellectual freedom, as we understand it, was repugnant to Plato.[3] In the *Republic* he advocates government censorship of the stories mothers tell their children, and proposes to banish poets altogether from Utopia. Had there been librarians in his time, he may have expelled them along with the poets, or found tasks for them fundamentally different from those we customarily associate with librarianship. In his last work, the *Laws,* he proposes strict government control of texts that schoolchildren will be permitted to read, since some authors had already bequeathed to the Greeks "writings of a dangerous character." Plato seems to abandon this troublesome topic with embarrassed haste, as if it awakened in him some painful conflict for which he could find no satisfactory resolution. The topic was to prove even more troublesome to the Renaissance Platonists, who found it necessary to explain away their master's scandalous strictures on poetry and writing in general, because they could not defend forthrightly a position that subverted their own passionate interest in the whole of Greek literature.

The foregoing is prologue, to underscore the fact that philosophers are not necessarily champions of intellectual freedom. The dogmatic ones are likely to be its worst enemies, equipped with subtle arguments to overthrow any position lacking a sound philosophical foundation.

We leap now across two millennia to the distinguished Spanish philosopher José Ortega y Gasset, and his celebrated speech "The Mission of the Librarian," delivered to an international congress of librarians in 1935. It is a provocative speech, packed with wisdom and full of philosophical concern for librarianship, and it concludes with a dramatic call to action that has thus far gone unheeded, despite its great emotional appeal. The text has proved to be extraordinarily popular, and is widely available in English, French, Spanish, and other languages. But the Spanish version in Ortega's *Obras Completas* is indispensable, for there you will find an epilogue, "Qué es un Libro,"[4] dropped from the speech and from the English translation of it, that lays bare the philosophical foundation of Ortega's peculiar notions about the mission of the librarian. The epilogue turns out to be a sympathetic rehashing of Plato's condemnation of writing in the *Phaedrus,* and plainly shows that Ortega, in his speech, is merely extending to librarianship the Platonic feeling about books. With the help of Plato, Ortega has found a proper place for librarians in Utopia.

[3] From Diogenes Laertius's *Lives of Eminent Philosophers* we learn that "Aristoxenus in his *Historical Notes* affirms that Plato wished to burn all the writings of Democritus that he could collect, but that Amyelas and Clinias the Pythagoreans prevented him, saying that there was no advantage in doing so, for already the books were widely circulated. And there is clear evidence for this in the fact that Plato, who mentions almost all the early philosophers, never once alludes to Democritus, not even where it would be necessary to controvert him, obviously because he knew that he would have to match himself against the prince of philosophers. . . ."

[4] José Ortega y Gasset, *Obras Completas,* Vol. 5 (Madrid: Revista de Occidente, 1964), pp. 230-34.

The concept of "mission" is central to Ortega's philosophy. "A mission is just this: the consciousness that every man has of his most authentic being, of that which he is called upon to realize." And a professional mission is that which it is *necessary* for professionals to do, whether any choose to do it or not. There is nothing casual about Ortega's decision to call his speech "The *Mission* of the Librarian."

As the necessities of the library profession have changed over the centuries, the mission of the librarian has accordingly changed. In the fifteenth century, Ortega avers, the mission consisted chiefly in gathering in the harvest of the printing press. By the nineteenth century the proliferation of books adds a new necessity: the need to catalog them. But the book is already beginning to lose what Ortega styles its original character of "pure facility," and in the twentieth century the book takes on a negative character, as an instrument in revolt against its creator. "The fully negative character," says Ortega, "surges up when an instrument created as a facility spontaneously provokes an unforeseen difficulty and aggressively turns upon man." Pursuing the metaphor of the book turned rebel, Ortega proposes a radical shift in the mission of the librarian:

> Here then is the point at which I see the new mission of the librarian rise up incomparably higher than all those preceding. Up until the present, the librarian has been principally occupied with the book as a thing, as a material object. From now on he must give his attention to the book as a living function. He must become a policeman, master of the raging book.

The necessities that require librarians to become policemen are then summed up:

> There are already too many books. Even when we drastically reduce the number of subjects to which man must direct his attention, the quantity of books that he must absorb is so enormous that it exceeds the limits of his time and his capacity of assimilation. Merely the work of orienting oneself in the bibliography of a subject today represents a considerable effort for an author and proves to be a total loss. For once he has completed that part of his work, the author discovers that he cannot read all that he ought to read. This leads him to read too fast and to read badly; it moreover leaves him with an impression of powerlessness and failure, and finally skepticism towards his own work.

(A paradox lies in this lament, for if there are indeed too many books, the problem would be self-adjusting if authors spent the proper time in bibliographical orientation and reading. Ortega, whose own works are voluminous, might at least have stopped writing, just as Plato should never have started if he really valued his own advice. Appealing as we may find the philosophical assurance that there are already too many books, the assertion will not bear logical scrutiny, since as yet we have no criterion of what constitutes "enough" books.) Ortega continues:

It is not only that there are too many books; they are being produced every day in torrential abundance. Many of them are useless and stupid; their existence and their conservation is a dead weight upon humanity.... At the same time, it also happens that in all disciplines one often regrets the absence of certain books, the lack of which holds up research....The excess and the lack of books are of the same origin: production is carried on without regimen, almost completely abandoned to spontaneous chance.

Here the peroration begins, and the mystery of the library-policeman's role in Utopia is cleared up. "Is it too Utopian," Ortega asks,

to imagine in a not too distant future librarians held responsible by society for the regulation of the production of books, in order to avoid the publication of superfluous ones and, on the other hand, to guard against the lack of those demanded by the complex of vital problems in every age?... It seems to me that the hour has arrived for the collective organization of book production; for the book itself, as a human modality, this organization is a matter of life and death.

And let no one offer me the foolish objection that such an organization would be an attack upon liberty. Liberty has not come upon the face of the earth to wring the neck of common sense.... The collective organization of book production has nothing to do with the subject of liberty, no more nor less than the need which has demanded the regulation of traffic in great cities of today. Moreover, the organization would not be of an authoritarian character, no more, in fact, than the internal organization of works in a good academy of sciences.

What are we to make of a *philosopher* who can see no distinction between regulating traffic in ideas and in automobiles? Who blandly asserts that regimentation need not be authoritarian? Who tells us there are both too many books and too few, when he cannot tell us how many is enough? One senses in Ortega the panic that wells up in a scholar as he discovers the astronomical dimensions of the bibliographical universe. And the attendant Utopian urge to return to a more primitive state of society, where philosophers can banish poets, and librarians will banish books. As Ortega sees it, a library is, or ought to be, principally an office of government censorship.

Most of what I have quoted from Ortega appeared (as excerpts from the speech) in the January, 1936 issue of the *Wilson Bulletin for Librarians*. In the same issue Stanley Kunitz delivered a stinging rebuke to Ortega that still makes lively reading. Here is the opening paragraph:

Of what were the librarians at Madrid, the sachems and hierarchs of the profession, in international congress assembled, thinking—did they stir uneasily in their seats—while José Ortega y Gasset, who has been called "one of the twelve peers of European thought," delivered his denunciation of the book? Reading his argument ... I wondered whether any in that assemblage had the impulse or, what is more, the courage, when the speaker had finished, to stand up and defend the book against its detractors. I suppose not. Convention audiences are notoriously phlegmatic; and, besides, communication with an international audience is difficult in any one language. Perhaps there was not a handful of librarians present who realized that their famous guest was calmly engaged in justifying their annihilation.

Later issues of the *Bulletin* also carried comment favorable to Ortega's position, whether from librarians who actually shared his philosophy, or suffered unmanageable cataloging backlogs, it is difficult to say.

Ortega's entire address (minus the epilogue) appeared in English translation twice in 1961,[5] but the republication of this astonishing speech drew no audible response from American librarians. Perhaps events in Hitler's Germany and Stalin's Russia are regarded as sufficient commentary on Ortega's preposterous program. But the need still persists for some alternative to the philosophy out of which it grew, and I will propose one here while discussing the mission of the librarian from the point of view of a librarian who is neither dismayed by the multiplicity of books nor awed by the pronouncements of philosophers.

My general attitude towards books is simply that of Friar Laurence toward living things:

> For naught so vile upon the earth doth live,
> But to the earth some special good doth give.

There are probably, as Ortega says, many "stupid" books in the world, and more are surely on the way. But a useless one (in the absolute sense) is unimaginable. Even a penny-dreadful is useful as a bad example, and as a testament to the kind of civilization that produced it. Judgment is needed only to determine how many bad examples any one library may usefully collect.

A book may contain things foolish, disgusting, appalling; a library of any size *must.* You may with constant vigilance and ceaseless toil keep weeds, insects, and serpents out of your garden plot, but a forest is something else. So are libraries, and we need the ecological good sense of Friar Laurence to restrain us from the righteous effort to purge them of all things vile.

As for the mission of the librarian, I believe it is still primarily the making of libraries, and this is a task incomparably higher than sitting like some Juno cross-legged over the nativity of books. To be sure there have been librarians willing to let others make libraries for them—college faculties, for example—but this implies only that some members of a profession may choose not to do what it is necessary that they do. By letting others make libraries for them, they escape those personal dangers that beset a librarian who takes his mission seriously.

[5] José Ortega y Gasset, "The Mission of the Librarian," tr. James Lewis and Ray Carpenter, *Antioch Review,* XXI, 2 (Summer, 1961), 133-54. Reprinted as a separate article in 1961 by G. K. Hall.

One fruitful source of danger is a careless choice of metaphors to describe our libraries.

Consider the perils of publicly declaring that a library is a storehouse of knowledge. Someone will discover on the shelves a book that exhibits blatant, undeniable ignorance, and he will invite the librarian to throw it out because it plainly has no place in a storehouse of knowledge. At that point the librarian may find it is too late to change his metaphor, but he may have to change his job if he refuses to throw the book out.

Those who travel widely in the world of books may agree that a more realistic case can be made for describing a library as a "treasury of learning and ignorance," although that metaphor is unsuitable for use around fiscal officers. They expect something else for their money.

The disdain of ignorance is widespread but unwarranted. Consider for a moment one example of the special pleasure it can give. Pliny, in the eighth book of his *Natural History,* speaks of the achlis, "born in the island of Scandinavia and never seen in Rome, although many have told stories of it—an animal that is not unlike the elk but has no joint at the hock and consequently is unable to lie down but sleeps leaning against a tree." And how does one catch an achlis? The thing to do, says Pliny, is to cut some trees nearly through; and when the achlis leans against one to go to sleep, down come tree and achlis together, the achlis no more able than the tree to get up and run from you. While we are smiling at the quaint credulity of Pliny (who himself was always smiling at the quaint credulity of the Greeks), this sobering question invades our mirth: How would one go about proving the absolute *non*-existence of the achlis? We have been taken in before on matters of well-attested learning—Piltdown man, for example—and we may be equally vulnerable to matters of well-attested ignorance. Has anyone thought of sawing some trees nearly through, and returning the next morning to see what he may find?

The librarian, above all others in the republic of learning, has need of the great Sceptic formula "I suspend judgment" to guide (but not overpower) him in his professional mission. He may personally deny the achlis if he likes. But woe betide him if he undertakes to drive from his shelves the achlis or anything else simply because he denies its truth.

When the time comes to write a *Pseudodoxia Epidemica* of the twentieth century, the books of ignorance will be indispensable, while the works of truth will be useless. And whoever compiles that enormous record of our false beliefs may discover that, through the alchemy of the decades, thousands upon thousands of books prematurely celebrated for their truth have grown strangely ridiculous; while other books, despised or neglected at their first appearance in the world, will be cherished for their late-blooming wisdom.

The accumulation of recorded error proceeds at about the pace at which we discover new knowledge, and the size of our libraries testifies as much to the magnitude of our ignorance as of our learning. Who would wish it otherwise? Man is a creature too readily disposed to erect imposing monuments commemorative of his own imagined grandeur. He needs large libraries to remind him of his real and imposing ignorance. Once more, an argument no one would think of presenting to the holders of the purse strings.

What argument then should be made, and what metaphor should be used to justify the librarian's mission as maker of libraries? Before attempting any case at all, one might profitably study Sextus Empiricus, the codifier of Sceptic philosophy, and see what Scepticism offers in the way of a philosophical foundation for the making of libraries.[6]

It is obvious to all of us that a library is a place in which thoughtful people search for something. But it is not obvious what kind of thinkers librarians can reasonably hope to accommodate. Sextus can help here, with the Sceptic discovery that every thinker must fall into one of three categories. First, there are those who affirm that the truth exists, and that they are already in full possession of it, so their search has reached its end. There is no point in making libraries for this group—the dogmatists—for they will eventually find reason to burn them down. A case in point is the great library at Alexandria, which, after a thousand years' glorious existence, was consigned to the flames at the command of a powerful dogmatist, the Caliph Umar bin al Khattab. To him one Amr bin al 'Ass wrote asking what should be done with the books in that marvelous library. The Caliph replied, "As for the books you mention, if their contents agree with the Book of God, then having the Book of God we are wealthy without them; and if they contradict the Book of God we have no need for them, so start destroying them." Which 'Amr bin al 'Ass did, distributing them throughout Alexandria to be burned in fireplaces. So great was the collection of books in that magnificent library that six months were required to burn them all up. It is said that when the Caliph was told what had happened, he was pleased.[7]

Seldom is the logic of the Alexandrian dilemma pushed to so ruthless and absolute a conclusion, but the light from that disastrous fire should at least help us to see what is going on, and where we may be heading, when librarians are implored or compelled to remove books from libraries because they oppose some popular dogma.

The second category of thinkers contains those who deny the possibility of knowing the truth about anything, and therefore assert that it

[6] The best introduction to Scepticism is Sextus himself. Philip Hallie's excellent edition of his selected writings, entitled *Scepticism, Man & God* (Middletown: Wesleyan University Press, 1964), presents the Sceptic approach with admirable conciseness.

[7] Zeydan, George, "The Burning of the Books at the Library of Alexandria and Elsewhere," in Edward Alexander Parsons, *The Alexandrian Library* ... (London: Cleaver-Hume, 1952), p. 414.

is sheer vanity even to begin the search. No need to build libraries for them, for at best they will not use them, and at worst they will decry the wasteful expenditure of public funds on useless institutions.

In the third category belong those who persevere in the search for truth, people who in Sextus's time, and long before, were known as Sceptics: a term that literally means "inquirers, searchers." Sceptics have been perversely misunderstood throughout the centuries as being philosophers who doubt and deny everything, thus paralyzing every effort to think and act rightly. The stigma is undeserved. For the avowed aim of the Sceptics was to free men from the absurd doctrines of the dogmatists by showing that for every dogma, one could find another dogma of equal weight in opposition to it. And in the face of conflicting dogmas, the Sceptic "suspends judgment" on both, passes judgment on neither, and calmly goes his own way.

If Heraclitus maintains that you cannot step in the same river twice, since all things are always changing; and if Parmenides informs you that nothing in fact changes since motion is logically impossible; then you suspend judgment on the point in dispute, walk or stand still as you please, and continue to study the enigma of motion if you are so disposed.[8] If Plato assures you the written word is useless while speech is perfect for teaching; and if Cratylus comes along and advises you to give up speech for any purpose whatever, since speaker, listener, and words are all changing even in the act of utterance; then you suspend judgment on the philosophical issue and talk, write, or hold your peace, according to the dictates of your common sense. Through suspension of judgment on non-evident matters, the Sceptic achieved the mental tranquillity that permitted him to function sensibly according to the laws, customs, and faith of his people—and to continue his philosophical inquiries.

Neither dogmatist nor nihilist can tolerate philosophically the Babel of books we call libraries. But a Sceptic relishes the conflict of fact, idea, and opinion that goes on in them, for the conflict keeps open for him a way to persevere in his search. Search for what? Search for the truth about himself, and about the universe. If this is so—and in Sceptic fashion I go no farther than proposing that it appears to me at the moment to be so—then what we should try to give this searcher is a library that can metaphorically be called

---

[8] I have chosen here for purposes of illustration a philosophical issue that looks innocent enough on its surface, if not indeed silly; but it underlies every serious defense of totalitarianism, beginning with Plato's *Republic*. Plato, troubled by the Heraclitean dogma of change and decay, concluded that the decline of governments and civilizations came about by their gradual departure from the Ideal Form in which they began. The natural (and, to Plato, wholesome) corrective to this process is to establish a totalitarian society in which the rulers, by means of force and fraud, would completely arrest political and social change. The ruling class will always rule, and the slave will always slave. The stability of such a society naturally depends upon the ruthless suppression of all statements critical of the rulers or their methods. While a Sceptic would abstain from debating the philosophical position adopted by totalitarianism, he would not hesitate to point out the self-evident suffering of its victims.

a mirror of the universe, a reflector of things that may appear true or false, pious or blasphemous, beautiful or ugly, depending on who is looking in the mirror.

I have stolen the metaphor from Shakespeare, who tells us that the function of drama is "to hold as 'twere the mirror up to nature; to show virtue her own feature, scorn her own image, and the very age and body of the time his form and pressure." If drama can do these things, a library can surely do as much and more—as is self-evident in that libraries contain dramas, whereas no drama can contain what is in our libraries.

Must a library hold all, or most of the books in the world, to reflect the universe entirely? I think not. Even a tiny mirror held at a distance from a huge object will still reflect the whole object, although not in such minute detail as a larger mirror would if held closer. The aim is what counts. If one is careful and resolute in the making of a modest-sized library, and goes about the task undogmatically, it will faithfully mirror the whole cosmic panorama of order and confusion, of grandeur and triviality.

The flood of books makes the task not impossible, but more engaging. The odds against complete success should be no cause for discouragement. Physicians struggle against disease knowing that all their patients will die anyhow; lawyers try cases in court knowing they will lose half of them; librarians can, if they will, make libraries that accurately reflect most that is known or believed about man and the universe.

The opportunity to attempt the making of such libraries is unique, or nearly so, in the history of librarianship. It grew out of our national experiment with human freedom, begun two centuries ago; and in some measure the success of that uncertain experiment will depend upon what American librarians make of their unusual opportunity. Frederick Jackson Turner, in that prophetic book called *The Frontier in American History,* forewarned that the strains upon our open society would grow as we moved away in time from the closing of the frontier, a place where a man could always strike out for himself and re-establish an open society when he found his community growing intolerant of his personal ideals. The geographical frontier is closed for good. But hopefully an American who finds his society closing down on him today can still strike out for the library, with some expectation of finding there, if nowhere else, an open intellectual society, a frontier of thought and feeling with boundaries wide enough to accommodate all the voices of dissent that keep alive our imperiled experiment in human freedom. Russia has lately shown us what the regimentation of book production can do to contract those boundaries and make libraries into conduits for whatever political, academic, or moral dogma is in vogue. Sceptical philosophy lights the way to make something far nobler of them.

A problem universe requires problem libraries. Making them is the most demanding and the most awkward necessity of the librarian's mission, since in the nature of things libraries must contain many books that offend our neighbors and ourselves. The offense will not be lessened by pretending that libraries are labyrinths of properly authorized learning. To develop the nerve to give the unavoidable offense, and to justify their position when offense is taken, librarians need a philosophy for their mission that can accommodate all dogmas by assenting to none. And those who use libraries likewise require a philosophy to enable them to see what a library is in its perfected state: a mirror of the universe; and what it must become if placed in the control of censors: an instrument of indoctrination. Scepticism is the name of the philosophy that justifies the librarian's mission, and answers the question, What is a library?

# II

# PRACTICE

# Introduction

A time limit is suggested at the beginning of each of these exercises, and there will ordinarily be no reason for you to exceed it, even if this means leaving some part of the exercise unfinished. Labor has no less need of moderation than indolence. Whenever some particular question or part of an exercise cannot be managed in a reasonable compass of time, leave it unfinished and return to it later if you have not already reached the time limit for the exercise. Failure to solve a particular problem in due time may result from either of two causes: your library lacks the required book; or, your search strategy is defective. The latter will more likely be the case, and if you suspect that it is, then review the pertinent chapter of the text, read the instructions for the exercise again, and attempt to solve the problem once more. If difficulties remain, then consult your instructor. The chief penalty you will suffer from inadequate performance of these exercises will come later in your academic career, should you then find yourself unable to use the library's resources efficiently. *Everyone should therefore endeavor to invigorate himself by reason and reflection, and determine to exert the latent force that nature may have reposited in him, before the hour of exigence comes upon him, and compulsion tortures him to diligence* (Dr. Johnson).

# *Exercise*
# 1
# Authentication of Facts

The source of certain statements of fact in Chapter 1 has been deliberately omitted. Choose any five of these unauthenticated statements of fact and attempt to locate books in the library which will either confirm or, possibly, refute these statements. Do not use a general encyclopedia *(Britannica, Americana,* etc.) for this assignment. When you have found a source for a factual statement, identify it as well as you are able without making any further effort to learn more than you already know about the formal techniques of identifying books. Do not exceed the time limit of 90 minutes, and do not call on anyone else for help with the assignment. The intent of the assignment is simply to *introduce* you directly to some of the problems of bibliographical practice, not to make you proficient in their solution; that proficiency will come in the execution of the assignments that lie ahead.

**Time: 90 minutes**

1. Fact: _____

_____

Source: _____

_____

2. Fact: _____

_____

Source: _____

_____

3. Fact: _____

_____

Source: _____

_____

Name _____ Date _____

4. Fact: _____

_____

    Source: _____

_____

5. Fact: _____

_____

    Source: _____

_____

Name _____ Date _____

# *Exercise*
# 2.1
# Bibliography Forms

[Before starting this exercise, read carefully Chapters 1 and 2 of Part I.] Go to the subject catalog and, in the upper left-hand corner of a standard 3 x 5 bibliography card, write the call number of *one* of the books that the library owns under each subject heading listed below. (You may discover in the case of some of these headings that the library owns no books concerning them.) When you have finished copying call numbers, then arrange your cards in the order of their call numbers, starting with numbers in class A (if there are any) and proceeding through class Z.[1] Then go to the shelves and make a complete bibliography citation for each book whose call number has been copied on one of the cards. (By having your cards pre-arranged in call-number order, you may save yourself about a mile's walk through the bookstacks.) Make your citations in pencil so corrections can be conveniently made when necessary. Return each book to the exact spot on the shelf where you found it after making your citation, because other students will need to see it too.[2] (Ordinarily librarians prefer that you do *not* reshelve books, but in this instance an exception seems necessary.) Whenever you are unable to locate a book readily, write "can't find" on the card and go on to other books that you can find. If you have not exceeded the time limit for the exercise after citing all the books that you can find, you might then attempt to locate the missing books, but not otherwise. Do not in any case make your citation from a catalog card: make it either with the book in hand, or not at all.

Here is a sample entry that you might make on a bibliography card for the subject heading "Alphabet":

PJ
4589
D5
     Diringer, David. *The Story of the Aleph Beth.*
     New York: Thomas Yoseloff, 1960.

[1] Dewey class numbers 000 through 999
[2] Disregard this instruction if advised to do so by your teacher.

Name  ———————————————  Date  ———————————————

Your completed file of cards will constitute a very sketchy, classified bibliography of the field of bibliography. The procedures you have gone through in compiling this card file are fundamental to any literature search, and you will often repeat them in gathering materials preparatory to writing a term paper. You should therefore learn to execute them swiftly and correctly, thus saving time that can be profitably spent in reading and reflecting on the contents of books. While your card file is limited, for the purposes of this exercise, to entries for books, a file that you might compile for the writing of a term paper would usually include cards for periodical articles and other types of materials as well, but the principles of their preparation would be the same: call number in the upper left-hand corner of the card and a complete formal citation of the work in the center.

**Time: 3 hours**

Selected List of Subject Headings in the Field of Bibliography

Alphabet
Alphabets
Bibliography
Bibliography—Best books
Bibliography—Bibliography
Bibliography—Early printed books—16th century
Bibliography—Rare books
Book collecting
Book collectors
Book design
Book industries and trade
Book ornamentation
Book selection
Bookbinding
Books
Books and reading
Calligraphers
Cataloging
Catalogs, Classified

Name _____ Date _____

Classification—Books
Classification, Decimal
Classification, Library of Congress
Copyists
Criticism, Textual
English language—Phonetics
Gutenberg, Johann, 1397?-1468
Hebrew language—Alphabet
Hieroglyphics
Illumination of books and manuscripts
Illustration of books
Imprints (in books)
Incunabula
Initials
Lettering
Libraries and readers
Manuscripts
Marbling (Bookbinding)
Miniature painting
Paleography
Paper
Paper making and trade
Pastedowns
Phonetic alphabet
Phonetics
Printers' marks
Printing
Printing—Dictionaries
Printing—History
Printing—Specimens
Printing, Practical
Printing, Practical—Style manuals
Printing press
Runes
Subject headings
Title page
Type and typefounding
Typesetting
Watermarks
Writing

Name ———————————— Date ————————————

A concluding question (to be answered on the last card in your file): You may have now discovered that the library does not own books for some of the subject headings listed above. Does this mean that the library has no information on those subjects? Explain.

Name _____ Date _____

# *Exercise*
# 2.2
# Footnote Forms

Select twenty-five of the bibliography citations you made in Exercise 2.1 and write them in the correct form for footnote citations, assuming in each instance that the footnote reference is to page 25 of the text you cite.

Example:

¹David Diringer, *The Story of the Aleph Beth* (New York: Thomas Yoseloff, 1960), p. 25.

**Time: 1 hour**

1. _____

_____

2. _____

_____

3. _____

_____

4. _____

_____

5. _____

_____

6. _____

_____

Name _____ Date _____

7. _____

_____

_____

8. _____

_____

_____

9. _____

_____

_____

10. _____

_____

_____

11. _____

_____

_____

12. _____

_____

_____

13. _____

_____

_____

14. _____

_____

_____

15. _____

_____

_____

16. _____

_____

_____

17. _____

_____

_____

18. _____

_____

_____

19. _____

_____

_____

Name _____ Date _____

20. _____
_____
_____

21. _____
_____
_____

22. _____
_____
_____

23. _____
_____
_____

24. _____
_____
_____

25. _____
_____
_____

Name _____  Date _____

# *Exercise*
# 3.1
# Subject-Heading Forms

Place a check mark beside each of the forms listed below that is used by the Library of Congress as a subject heading. To determine which forms are subject headings, and which are not, you will have to check each form on this list against the Library of Congress's official list of subject headings, copies of which you should find near the subject catalog.

**Time: 30 minutes**

Abbeys
Absence and presumption of death
Absolutism

[Note that this is *not* a subject heading. It is a form from which a see-reference has been made to another synonymous term which *is* used as a subject heading. The fact that it is a see-reference and not a subject heading is indicated by the statement "Absolutism. *See* Despotism." This is a brief way of saying "If you are looking for a book on the subject of absolutism, you may find it entered under 'Despotism,' but you will certainly not find it under 'Absolutism,' since that term is not used as a subject heading in the catalog."]

Accidents—Psychological aspects
Air pollution
Binding of books
Biography, writing of
Church and state
Church and war
Cobalt amines
Concentration camps
Conjuring

Name _____ Date _____

Discoveries (in geography)
Drama, Ancient
Drama, Classical
Environment
Fighting (Psychology)
Fighting, Hand-to-hand
Government spending policy
Government support of science, literature, and art
Hinduism—Sacred books
Hornpipe (Dance)
Horoscope
Horror
Integration in education
Music
Music—Acoustics and physics
Music—Study and teaching
Music, Ancient
Music, Primitive
Music as a profession
Music in prisons
Music of the spheres

[Note carefully the filing sequence of the eight preceding headings. First there is the single noun "Music"; then its subdivisions follow, arranged alphabetically; then the noun with the adjective in the inverted position, arranged alphabetically by the adjective; and finally the phrase forms, arranged alphabetically by the words in the phrase. Since this pattern of arrangement applies to all other subject headings as well, you should keep it in mind when using the subject catalog.]

U. S.—History
U. S.—History—Fiction
U. S.—History—Maps
U. S.—History—Study and teaching
U. S.—History—Colonial period
U. S.—History—Revolution—Biography
U. S.—History—Civil War—Poetry
U. S.—History—20th century
U. S.—History—European War, 1914-1918
U. S.—History—1919-1933

[Notice the arrangement of the ten headings above, beginning with "U. S. — History." There is first a sequence of form or topic subdivisions (Fiction, Maps,

Name _____ Date _____

Study and teaching) arranged alphabetically; then there follows a sequence of historical period subdivisions (Colonial period, and so on), arranged chronologically by the period, *not alphabetically*. This principle of arranging the subdivisions of the heading "History" first by topic, alphabetically, and then by period, chronologically, is also followed elsewhere in the catalog for the history of other nations. Unless you remember these facts of catalog arrangement, you will find it extremely difficult, if not impossible, to locate books on history through the subject catalog.]

War (International law)
War and Christianity
War propaganda
Water pollution
Water-supply, Industrial
Woman—Defense
Woman—Emancipation
Women as astronauts
Women in the Armed Forces
Zither music

Name ＿＿＿＿＿＿＿＿＿＿＿＿ Date ＿＿＿＿＿＿＿＿＿

# Exercise
## 3.2
# Subject-Headings: See-Also References

Listed below is a sample group of subject headings, some of which have see-also references cited in the Library of Congress list and others which do not. Beside those which do not, place an X. For those which do, cite the heading on a separate sheet of paper and list under it all the see-also references that you find in the Library of Congress list.[1] When you have done this, take your list of see-also references to the subject catalog and check to see which, if any, of the subject headings *referred to* are in the catalog. Place a check mark beside those that you find, and leave the others unmarked.

**Time: 90 minutes**

Chorales
Climatology
Commandments, Ten
Condemned books
Courts and courtiers
Dancing mice
Detectives in literature
Didactic literature
Emblems, National
English language—Alphabet
English language—Idioms, corrections, errors
Extrasensory perception
Fees, Professional
Feudalism
Foreign exchange
Fungi, Pathogenic

[1] In the Library of Congress list the see-also references are those terms listed beside and immediately below the designation *sa.* Ignore all terms listed after the designations *x* and *xx.*

Name _____ Date _____

Games, Theory of
Geology, Stratigraphic—Cenozoic
Illumination of books and manuscripts
Inflation (Finance)
Printing—History
Type and type-founding
Unemployed
Water—Pollution
Woman—Legal status, laws, etc.

Name _____ Date _____

*Exercise*
# 3.3
# Subject-Headings

Choose any *one* of the subject headings below and develop a list of a hundred subject headings related to it. This can be done most easily by listing all the see-also references you find under the heading you choose, and continuing to trace all subsequent see-also references that are made from this first group of see-also references.

**Time: 1 hour**

Social ethics
Political ethics
Cost and standard of living
Economic policy
Negligence
Motors
Creation (Literary, artistic, etc.)
Evolution
Woman
Man
Books
Minorities
Natural resources

Name _____ Date _____

# *Exercise*
# 3.4
## Subject-Headings

Assuming that you would like to find books that answer the descriptions listed below, write beneath each description the exact subject-heading form under which such a book would be entered in the subject catalog. Consult the subject-heading list first, and then, as necessary (especially for proper nouns) the subject catalog.

**Time: 90 minutes**

A bibliography of American literature.

———————————————————————————————

A study of Shakespeare's play *King Lear.*

———————————————————————————————

A book about the British in West Africa.

———————————————————————————————

A book about the foreign relations of Germany with the U. S.

———————————————————————————————

A book about frontier life in the American West.

———————————————————————————————

A book about cross-country journeys in the days of the American frontier.

———————————————————————————————

A French grammar.

———————————————————————————————

Name ————————————————  Date ————————————

A dictionary of American slang.

_____

An etymological dictionary of the English language.

_____

A history of science.

_____

A critical study of American literature of the colonial period.

_____

A book about science and religion.

_____

A book about the moral aspects of the atomic bomb.

_____

A collection of eighteenth-century English poems.

_____

A drama about the life of Napoleon.

_____

A book about slavery in the South.

_____

A book about the philosophy of chemistry.

_____

A book about chemists.

_____

A book about medicine as a profession.

_____

A book about government ownership of electric utilities.

_____


Name  _____  Date  _____

# Exercise
## 3.5
## Subject-Headings

Listed below are descriptions of books dealing with some aspect of the United States. Cite the exact subject-heading form under which each of these books would be entered, using either the subject catalog or the list of subject headings (or both) to determine the correct forms. (You will note that the pattern of these forms would be repeated for books dealing with countries other than the United States, so if you can find the correct form for the United States you should be able to find it for all other nations too.)

**Time: 1 hour**

A book about Negroes in the armed forces of the United States.

_____

A book about government documents of the United States.

_____

A book about moral conditions in the United States.

_____

A book about political corruption in the United States.

_____

A historical atlas of the United States.

_____

A book about postal service in the United States.

_____

Name  _____  Date  _____

A book about officials of the United States Government.

_____

A dictionary of American biography.

_____

A history of the American Revolution.

_____

A collection of source materials for the study of the colonial period of American history.

_____

A book about the draft in the United States.

_____

A book about fortifications of the United States.

_____

A collection of Civil War photographs.

_____

A book about Civil War prisons.

_____

A book about the first census of the United States.

_____

A book about American courts.

_____

A book about civil disobedience in the United States.

_____

A book about the literature of the United States.

_____

A book about the weather of the United States.

_____

A book about the discovery and exploration of the United States.

_____

Name _____ Date _____

# Publications Less than Book Length

Beside each title that your library owns, state its location (Reference Room, Periodical Room, Index Tables, etc.) and indicate the time period it covers.

**Time: 90 minutes**

*Alternative Press Index*
*Applied Science and Technology Index*
*Art Index*
*Bibliographic Index*
*Biography Index*
*Biological Abstracts*
*Book Review Digest*
*Book Review Index*
*Business Periodicals Index*
*Chemical Abstracts*
*Christian Science Monitor Subject Index*
*Education Index*
*Engineering Index*
*Environment Information Access*
*Essay and General Literature Index*
*Index to Book Reviews in the Humanities*
*Index to Little Magazines*
*Index to Periodical Articles By and About Negroes*
*Index to Poetry* (Granger)
*Index to Religious Periodical Literature*
*Library Literature*
*London Times Index*
*MLA International Bibliography of Books and Articles on Modern Languages
and Literatures*

Name _____ Date _____

*Music Index*
*New York Times Index*
*Physics Abstracts*
*Play Index*
*Poole's Index to Periodical Literature*
*Psychological Abstracts*
*Public Affairs Information Service Bulletin*
*Readers' Guide to Periodical Literature*
*Short Story Index*
*Social Sciences and Humanities Index*
*Sociological Abstracts*

Name _____ Date _____

# Exercise
## 4.2
# Publications Less than Book Length

Where citations are required, make them in the *correct bibliographic form,* insofar as this is possible using only the information that you find in the various indexes, etc., that you consult. Answer all questions and make all citations on this sheet.

**Time: 3 hours**

1. Cite one good book published in 1963 about cross-country journeys in the days of the American frontier.

_____

2. Who reviewed the book published in 1959 with the title *Buddhism in Chinese History?*

_____

3. Cite one essay (not a periodical article) published in 1963 on the subject of extrasensory perception.

_____

4. Cite one book (not a periodical) which contains an article about Richard Hakluyt.

_____

5. Who is the author of the short story "A Rose for Emily"?

_____

6. Who wrote the play *Archy and Mehitabel?*

_____

Name _____ Date _____

7. What periodical printed, in 1962, a reproduction of Henri Rousseau's painting "Le Rêve"?

_____

8. Cite a periodical article published in 1961 about student ratings of college professors.

_____

9. Cite the title of an essay (not a periodical article) published in 1960 about Bertrand Russell's book *Why I Am Not a Christian.*

_____

10. Cite the title of a short poem about Henry Purcell.

_____

11. Cite a popular periodical article published in 1961 on the therapeutic aspects of music.

_____

12. Cite a scholarly periodical article published in 1962 on the therapeutic aspects of music.

_____

13. What index is available to the contents of the *Saturday Review?*

_____

14. Cite one scholarly periodical article published in 1950 on the subject of German concentration camps.

_____

15. Cite one popular periodical article published in 1962 on the subject of German concentration camps.

_____

16. Cite one popular periodical article published in 1961 on the subject of Negro troops in the Civil War.

_____

Name _____ Date _____

# 5.1
# Classification of Books  [LC]

Beside the class numbers listed below, write the subjects to which they are assigned in the Library of Congress classification schedules. Place a check mark beside those classes in which you find one or more books shelved in the stacks.

**Time: 1 hour**

B407

BD331

BF1074

BL325

CJ391

CT3710

D114

D501

DA677

DK549

E457.909

F292N5

GC301

GR975

JC311

Name _____ Date _____

ML1011

NB92

PN6340

PR2807

PZ5

Q164

QA533

QB51.5

D511

Z1002

Name _____ Date _____

# Classification of Books [Dewey]

Beside the class numbers listed below, write the subjects to which they are assigned in the Dewey classification schedule. Place a check mark beside those classes in which you find one or more books shelved in the stacks.

**Time: 1 hour**

002

017.1

125

133.1

211.6

270.2

311.2

364.36

421.7

480

509

551.8

581.1

616.89

623.4

Name _____ Date _____

634.927

721

751.6

781.71

812

822

881

914

920.1

940.3

Name _____ Date _____

# *Exercise*
# 5.2
# Classification of Books

Beside the topics listed below, write the classification number (Dewey or Library of Congress, whichever your library uses) that has been assigned to each. First check the subject catalog to see if you can find enough entries on the subject to deduce from the call numbers what the class number probably is, and then cross-check it in the classification schedule. *Place a check mark beside those numbers which you find in this way.* You will have to consult the classification schedules (and their indexes) directly to locate the others.

**Time: 1 hour**

Inductive logic

Hypnotism

Biography of Abraham Lincoln

Revolutionary period of U. S. history

Higher education

Magnetism

Plant embryology

Medieval astronomy

Study and teaching of mathematics

Bibliography of Geoffrey Chaucer

General history of science

Protons (Physics)

Name ————————————————  Date ————————————————

Psychology of dreams

Astrology

Education of adults

Name _____ Date _____

# Exercise
## 6.1
# The Reference Collection [LC]

Listed below are descriptions of various kinds of reference books. Below each description, cite the *short title* (do not use the full form of bibliographical citations) of one book in your library that answers the description. Also note beside the title the designation of the major class to which it belongs (that is, the first line of letters in the call number only). While it will be beneficial for you to consider briefly the contents of these books, and to examine other reference books as well as the ones you list, you will not be obliged to do so for the purposes of this assignment. You will notice that this listing proceeds in classification sequence, beginning with a book in class A and ending with one in class V.

**Time: 90 minutes**

1. A general almanac.

_____

_____

2. A book of "firsts" in American history.

_____

_____

3. A dictionary of philosophy.

_____

_____

4. A dictionary of psychology.

_____

_____

5. An encyclopedia of witchcraft.

_____

_____

Name _____ Date _____

6. A dictionary of Buddhism.

_____

_____

7. An encyclopedia of religion.

_____

_____

8. A concordance to the Bible.

_____

_____

9. A biographical dictionary of saints.

_____

_____

10. A dictionary of the origins of Christian names.

_____

_____

11. A chronological outline of modern history.

_____

_____

12. A dictionary of European history.

_____

_____

13. A dictionary of British biography.

_____

_____

14. A dictionary of the classical world.

_____

_____

15. A dictionary of American history.

_____

_____

16. A dictionary of American biography.

_____

_____

Name _____ Date _____

17. A book of pictures of the American presidents.

_____

_____

18. A dictionary of American nicknames.

_____

_____

19. A "who's who" of Southerners.

_____

_____

20. A geographical dictionary.

_____

_____

21. A dictionary of American holidays, anniversaries, etc.

_____

_____

22. An encyclopedia of sports.

_____

_____

23. An encyclopedia of dance.

_____

_____

24. An encyclopedia of the social sciences.

_____

_____

25. An abstract of United States statistics.

_____

_____

26. An encyclopedia of real estate practice.

_____

_____

27. A biographical dictionary of American congressmen.

_____

_____

Name _____ Date _____

28. A directory of scholarships and student loans.

_____

_____

29. A dictionary of music and musicians.

_____

_____

30. A dictionary of composers.

_____

_____

31. A handbook of the opera.

_____

_____

32. An art encyclopedia.

_____

_____

33. A rhyming dictionary.

_____

_____

34. A thesaurus of the English language.

_____

_____

35. A dictionary of the English language in twelve volumes.

_____

_____

36. An encyclopedia of names.

_____

_____

37. A dictionary of slang.

_____

_____

38. A biographical dictionary of authors of various nations.

_____

_____

Name _____ Date _____

39. An index to poetry.

_____

_____

40. A collection of general quotations.

_____

_____

41. A collection of proverbs.

_____

_____

42. A handbook to the study of French literature.

_____

_____

43. A biographical dictionary of British authors.

_____

_____

44. A concordance to Shakespeare.

_____

_____

45. A dictionary of Shakespeare's bawdy terms.

_____

_____

46. A handbook to the study of American literature.

_____

_____

47. A biographical dictionary of American authors.

_____

_____

48. An encyclopedia of science.

_____

_____

49. A biographical dictionary of mathematicians.

_____

_____

Name _____ Date _____

50. A book of mathematical tables.

_____

_____

51. A biographical dictionary of chemists.

_____

_____

52. A dictionary of biology.

_____

_____

53. A book for identifying shrubs.

_____

_____

54. An encyclopedia of American birds.

_____

_____

55. A medical dictionary.

_____

_____

56. A hunting and fishing guide.

_____

_____

57. An automotive encyclopedia.

_____

_____

58. A dictionary of applied chemistry.

_____

_____

59. An encyclopedia of small arms.

_____

_____

60. A nautical dictionary.

_____

_____

Name _____ Date _____

# The Reference Collection [Dewey]

Listed below are descriptions of various kinds of reference books. Below each description, cite the *short title* (do not use the full form for bibliographical citations) of one book in your library that answers the description. Also note beside the title the designation of the *major* class to which it belongs (for example, 010, 110, 230, etc.). While it will be beneficial for you to consider briefly the contents of these books, and to examine other reference books as well as the ones you list, you will not be obliged to do so for the purposes of this assignment. You will notice that this listing proceeds in classification sequence, beginning with a book in the 000s and ending with one in the 900s. (If after one minute you have failed to locate any particular reference book, go on to the next, because it is possible that your library does not own the type specified.)

**Time: 90 minutes**

1. A book of "firsts" in American history.

_____

_____

2. A dictionary of philosophy.

_____

_____

3. An encyclopedia of witchcraft.

_____

_____

4. A dictionary of psychology.

_____

_____

5. An encyclopedia of religion.

_____

_____

Name _____ Date _____

6. A concordance to the Bible.

_____

_____

7. A dictionary of Buddhism.

_____

_____

8. An encyclopedia of the social sciences.

_____

_____

9. A general almanac.

_____

_____

10. An abstract of United States statistics.

_____

_____

11. A biographical dictionary of American congressmen.

_____

_____

12. An encyclopedia of real estate practice.

_____

_____

13. A nautical dictionary.

_____

_____

14. A directory of scholarships and student loans.

_____

_____

15. A dictionary of American holidays, anniversaries, etc.

_____

_____

16. A collection of proverbs.

_____

_____

Name _____ Date _____

17. A dictionary of the English language in twelve volumes.

_____

_____

18. A thesaurus of the English language.

_____

_____

19. A rhyming dictionary.

_____

_____

20. A dictionary of slang.

_____

_____

21. An encyclopedia of science.

_____

_____

22. A book of mathematical tables.

_____

_____

23. A dictionary of biology.

_____

_____

24. A book for identifying shrubs.

_____

_____

25. An encyclopedia of American birds.

_____

_____

26. A medical dictionary.

_____

_____

27. An encyclopedia of small arms.

_____

_____

Name _____ Date _____

28. An automotive encyclopedia.

_____

_____

29. A dictionary of applied chemistry.

_____

_____

30. An art encyclopedia.

_____

_____

31. A dictionary of music and musicians.

_____

_____

32. A handbook of the opera.

_____

_____

33. An encyclopedia of sports.

_____

_____

34. An encyclopedia of dance.

_____

_____

35. A hunting and fishing guide.

_____

_____

36. A biographical dictionary of authors of various nations.

_____

_____

37. An index to poetry.

_____

_____

38. A collection of general quotations.

_____

_____

Name _____ Date _____

39. A handbook to the study of American literature.

_____

_____

40. A concordance to Shakespeare.

_____

_____

41. A dictionary of Shakespeare's bawdy terms.

_____

_____

42. A handbook to the study of French literature.

_____

_____

43. A chronological outline of modern history.

_____

_____

44. A geographical dictionary.

_____

_____

45. A dictionary of the classical world.

_____

_____

46. A dictionary of British biography.

_____

_____

47. A dictionary of American biography.

_____

_____

48. A "who's who" of Southerners.

_____

_____

49. A biographical dictionary of saints.

_____

_____

Name _____ Date _____

50. A book of pictures of the American presidents.

_____

_____

51. A biographical dictionary of mathematicians.

_____

_____

52. A biographical dictionary of chemists.

_____

_____

53. A dictionary of composers.

_____

_____

54. A biographical dictionary of American authors.

_____

_____

55. A biographical dictionary of British authors.

_____

_____

56. A dictionary of the origins of Christian names.

_____

_____

57. A dictionary of American nicknames.

_____

_____

58. An encyclopedia of names.

_____

_____

59. A dictionary of European history.

_____

_____

60. A dictionary of American history.

_____

_____

Name _____ Date _____

# *Exercise*
# 6.2
# The Bibliography Collection [LC]

Listed below are descriptions of various kinds of bibliographies. Under each description, cite the *short title* (do not use the full form for bibliographical citations) of one book in the collection that answers to the description. You will notice that this listing proceeds in classification sequence, so you should be able to discover the appropriate titles by simply reading the shelves.

**Time: 1 hour**

1. A bibliography of bibliographies appearing in books and journal articles.

———————————————————————————————————

2. A listing of the world's "best" books.

———————————————————————————————————

3. A bibliography of anonymous and pseudonymous English literature.

———————————————————————————————————

4. A record of books published in the United States, 1820-1861.

———————————————————————————————————

5. A record of books published in the United States in 1776.

———————————————————————————————————

6. A digest of book reviews published in 1942.

———————————————————————————————————

7. A guide to publications of the United States government.

———————————————————————————————————

Name ——————————————————— Date ———————————————

8. A dictionary of contemporary American authors and their writings.

_____

9. A bibliography of American literature.

_____

10. A bibliography of the American novel.

_____

11. A bibliography of bibliographies of American history.

_____

12. A comprehensive bibliography of English literature.

_____

13. A bibliography of British history.

_____

14. A bibliography of biography.

_____

15. A bibliography of drama.

_____

16. A bibliography of education.

_____

17. A bibliography of short stories.

_____

18. A bibliography of travel literature.

_____

19. A bibliography of periodicals.

_____

20. A bibliography of newspapers.

_____

21. A bibliography of Geoffrey Chaucer.

_____

Name _____ Date _____

22. A bibliography of James Joyce.

_____

23. A bibliography of William Shakespeare.

_____

24. A bibliography of William Wordsworth.

_____

Name _____ Date _____

# Exercise
## 6.21
# The Bibliography Collection [Dewey]

Listed below are descriptions of various kinds of bibliographies. Using the subject catalog, attempt to locate *one* bibliography in the library that answers each description, and cite its *short title* under the description. Also, give the class number of each title that you locate in the catalog (e.g. 016.51, 510.16, etc.), writing the number immediately after the title.

**Time: 1 hour**

1. A bibliography of book reviews.

_____

2. A bibliography of U. S. government publications.

_____

3. A bibliography of the American novel.

_____

4. A bibliography of English drama.

_____

5. A bibliography of American history.

_____

6. A bibliography of education.

_____

7. A bibliography of William Shakespeare.

_____

Name _____ Date _____

8. A bibliography of botany.

_____

9. A bibliography of periodicals.

_____

10. A bibliography of physics.

_____


Now make a list of your ten class numbers, arranging them from the lowest to the highest. From your list, would you expect to find all bibliographies in your library shelved in fairly close proximity to each other, or scattered throughout the library? If the latter, what disadvantages (or advantages) do you perceive in such an arrangement?


Name _____ Date _____

# Exercise
## 6.3
# The Reference Collection

A. Cite book, chapter, and verse for the following Biblical passages.

**Time: 20 minutes**

1. Let every man be swift to hear, slow to speak, slow to wrath.

_____

2. Stolen waters are sweet, and bread eaten in secret is pleasant.

_____

3. Whoso loveth instruction loveth knowledge: but he that hateth reproof is brutish.

_____

4. A feast is made for laughter, and wine maketh merry: but money answereth all things.

_____

5. Of making many books there is no end: and much study is a weariness of the flesh.

_____

6. Take us the foxes, the little foxes, that spoil the vines: for our vines have tender grapes.

_____

7. A man shall be as an hiding place from the wind, and a covert from the tempest; as rivers of water in a dry place, as the shadow of a great rock in a weary land.

_____

Name _____ Date _____

8. Cast thy bread upon the waters: for thou shalt find it after many days.

_____

9. Remember now thy Creator in the days of thy youth, while the evil days come not, nor the years draw nigh, when thou shalt say, I have no pleasure in them.

_____

10. Where there is no vision, the people perish.

_____


B. Cite the title of the Shakespearean play in which each of the following lines appears.


**Time: 20 minutes**

_____

1. Nothing in his life became him like the leaving it.

_____

2. There's special providence in the fall of a sparrow.

_____

3. Alas, poor Yorick! I knew him, Horatio.

_____

4. It is a custom / More honour'd in the breach than the observance.

_____

5. How weary, stale, flat, and unprofitable / Seem to me all the uses of this world!

_____

6. Frailty, thy name is woman!

_____

7. Uneasy lies the head that wears a crown.

_____

Name _____ Date _____

8. We owe God a death. . . . No man's too good to serve's prince, and let it go which way it will, he that dies this year is quit for the next.

_____

9. The play's the thing / Wherein I'll catch the conscience of the king.

_____

10. Dost think because thou art virtuous, there shall be no more cakes and ale?

_____

C. Identify the authors of the following quotations.

**Time: 20 minutes**

1. Let me have music dying, and I seek / No more delight.

_____

2. Those oft are stratagems which errors seem, / Nor is it Homer nods, but we that dream.

_____

3. Better to reign in Hell, than serve in Heav'n.

_____

4. Had we but world enough and time, / This coyness, lady, were no crime.

_____

5. So hoote he lovede that by nyghtertale / He sleep namoore than dooth a nyghtyngale.

_____

6. Sownynge in moral vertu was his speche, / And glady wolde he lerne and gladly teche.

_____

Name _____ Date _____

7. He prayeth best who loveth best / All things both great and small.

_____

8. From harmony, from heavenly harmony, / This universal frame began.

_____

9. Art thou pale for weariness / Of climbing Heaven and gazing on the earth?

_____

10. Much have I travell'd in the realms of gold, / And many goodly states and kingdoms seen.

_____


D. What is the meaning (in English) of the following Latin phrases?

**Time: 10 minutes**

1. Ad astra per ardua.

_____

2. Post hoc, ergo propter hoc.

_____

3. Desinit in piscem mulier formosa superne.

_____

4. De profundis.

_____

5. Deo volente.

_____


Name _____ Date _____

*Exercise*
# 6.4
# The Reference Collection [LC]

Answer very briefly the following questions (the classification sequence of the reference books in which the answers can be found follows the order of the questions themselves; thus the answer to the first question will be found somewhere in class A, and the answer to the last question will be found in class V).

**Time: 3 hours**

1. When was the first singing telegram sung in the United States?

_____

2. What is unusual about the literary form of the Book of Lamentations?

_____

3. In heraldry, what is meant by an "escutcheon of pretence"?

_____

4. What do archaeologists mean by a "canopic jar"?

_____

5. What is the proper way to address a letter to the wife of the Lord Mayor of Dublin?

_____

6. What is the origin of the name Patrick?

_____

7. What historic event happened in Constantinople on May 29, 1453?

_____

Name _____ Date _____

8. How did it happen that the English playwright William Congreve continued to be fed after he died?

_____

9. Who was the father of the Greek warrior Odysseus?

_____

10. What is the meaning of *halizah* in Jewish tradition?

_____

11. What is the state bird of Louisiana?

_____

12. What American was known as "The Millionaire Hobo"?

_____

13. Of what American college was Wendell Melton Patton president in 1966?

_____

14. When Milton wrote the simile "Thick as autumnal leaves that strow the brooks/In Vallombrosa," what country was he writing about?

_____

15. What do folklorists mean by a "chain tale"?

_____

16. On what day is the feast of St. Agnes celebrated?

_____

17. What is the Dance of Death?

_____

18. What do social scientists mean by "conspicuous consumption"?

_____

19. How many murders were reported in the United States in 1970?

_____

20. What was the infant mortality rate of the white population in the United States in 1915? Of the nonwhite?

_____

Name _____        Date _____

21. In the world of finance, what is meant by "Lombard loans"?

_____

22. What is the address of the Greater Blouse and Skirt Contractors Association?

_____

23. What American university offers a Ph.D. program in folklore?

_____

24. What connection does Sir Roger de Coverly have with the world of music?

_____

25. What book contains a reproduction of Fra Filippo Lippi's painting called the "Dance of Salomé"?

_____

26. What caused the near-destruction of the Parthenon?

_____

27. What is the meaning of the Anglo-Saxon word *Middangeard?*

_____

28. Give four words that rhyme with "jealous."

_____

29. Give four synonyms for "marsh."

_____

30. What English play has a character in it named Lothario?

_____

31. What word is abbreviated *mss.?*

_____

32. What is the meaning of the American slang word *horsefeathers?*

_____

33. Name two characters in Walpole's novel *The Castle of Otranto.*

_____

Name _____ Date _____

34. Give the title of a poem about Julian the Apostate.

_____

35. Give the title of a poem by Stephen Duck.

_____

36. How did it happen that the Japanese playwright Kwanami wrote no plays?

_____

37. What is the origin of the name Mother Goose?

_____

38. What was the original title of *The Devil's Dictionary,* by the American author Ambrose Bierce?

_____

39. How was it that the great Irish mathematician William Rowan Hamilton could choose either August 3 or 4 as his birthday?

_____

40. Which constellation is known as "The Archer"?

_____

41. What do chemists mean by a "Baeyer reaction"?

_____

42. What is the scientific name for the flower Love-in-a-Mist?

_____

43. What is the scientific name of Darwin's finches?

_____

44. What is the scientific name of the Ornate Shrew?

_____

45. What is the medical use of the drug meprobamate?

_____

46. Name two ingredients of a formula for cleaning jewelry.

_____

Name _____ Date _____

47. Did Samuel Colt, the famous gunmaker, ever make a .45 calibre revolver?

_____

48. What is meant by the American military term *CONELRAD?*

_____

49. What is the usual marking on the tail of a Russian military airplane?

_____

50. In nautical language, what is a donkey engine?

_____

Name _____ Date _____

# Exercise
# 6.41
# The Reference Collection [Dewey]

Answer very briefly the following questions (the classification sequence of the reference books in which the answers can be found follows the order of the questions themselves; thus the answer to the first question will be found somewhere in class 016, and the answer to the last question will be found in class 929). If after five minutes you have not found the answer to a particular question, leave it unanswered and go on to the next.

**Time: 3 hours**

1. What book contains a reproduction of Fra Filippo Lippi's painting called the "Dance of Salomé"?

_____

2. When was the first singing telegram sung in the United States?

_____

3. What is the address of the Greater Blouse and Skirt Contractors Association?

_____

4. What is unusual about the literary form of the Book of Lamentations?

_____

5. What is the meaning of *halizah* in Jewish tradition?

_____

6. What do social scientists mean by "conspicuous consumption"?

_____

Name _____ Date _____

7. How many murders were reported in the United States in 1970?

_____

8. What was the infant mortality rate of the white population of the United States in 1915? Of the nonwhite?

_____

9. In the world of finance, what is meant by "Lombard loans"?

_____

10. What is meant by the American military term *CONELRAD?*

_____

11. In nautical language, what is a donkey engine?

_____

12. What American university offers a Ph.D. program in folklore?

_____

13. On what day is the feast of St. Agnes celebrated?

_____

14. What is the proper way to address a letter to the wife of the Lord Mayor of Dublin?

_____

15. What do folklorists mean by a "chain tale"?

_____

16. What word is abbreviated *mss.?*

_____

17. Give four synonyms for "marsh."

_____

18. Give four words that rhyme with "jealous."

_____

19. What is the meaning of the Anglo-Saxon word *middangeard?*

_____


Name_____ Date_____

20. Which constellation is known as "The Archer"?

___

21. What do chemists mean by a "Baeyer reaction"?

___

22. What is the scientific name for the flower Love-in-a-Mist?

___

23. What is the scientific name of the Ornate Shrew?

___

24. What is the scientific name of Darwin's finches?

___

25. What is the medical use of the drug meprobamate?

___

26. Did Samuel Colt, the famous gunmaker, ever make a .45 calibre revolver?

___

27. What is the usual marking on the tail of a Russian military airplane?

___

28. Name two ingredients of a formula for cleaning jewelry.

___

29. What caused the near-destruction of the Parthenon?

___

30. What connection does Sir Roger de Coverly have with the world of music?

___

31. How did it happen that the Japanese playwright Kwanami wrote no plays?

___

32. What is the Dance of Death?

___

Name_____ Date_____

33. Name two characters in Walpole's novel *The Castle of Otranto.*

_____

34. Give the title of a poem about Julian the Apostate.

_____

35. Give the title of a poem by Stephen Duck.

_____

36. What was the original title of *The Devil's Dictionary,* by the American author Ambrose Bierce?

_____

37. What is the origin of the name Mother Goose?

_____

38. What is the meaning of the American slang word *horsefeathers?*

_____

39. What historic event happened in Constantinople on May 29, 1453?

_____

40. When Milton wrote the simile "Thick as autumnal leaves that strow the brooks/In Vallombrosa," what country was he talking about?

_____

41. What do archaeologists mean by a "canopic jar"?

_____

42. Who was the father of the Greek warrior Odysseus?

_____

43. What is the state bird of Louisiana?

_____

44. How did it happen that the English playwright William Congreve continued to be fed after he died?

_____

Name _____ Date _____

45. Of what American college was Wendell Melton Patton president in 1966?

_____

46. How was it that the great Irish mathematician William Rowan Hamilton could choose either August 3 or 4 as his birthday?

_____

47. What is the origin of the name Patrick?

_____

48. What English play has a character in it named Lothario?

_____

49. What American was known as "The Millionaire Hobo"?

_____

50. In heraldry, what is meant by an "escutcheon of pretence"?

_____

Name _____ Date _____

# The Bibliography Collection [LC]

Answer briefly the following questions. The answers (or leads to answers) will be found in the Z collection, beginning with a book in class Z1045, and working forward.

**Time: 2 hours**

1. What author used the pseudonym Growley Byles?

2. Who is the author of the anonymously published work entitled *Fumifugium; or The Inconvenience of the Aer, and Smoake of London Dissipated; Together with Remedies Humbly Proposed* (1661)?

3. Cite one book published in the United States between 1858 and 1860.

4. Cite one book published in the United States between 1900 and 1905.

5. Cite one book published in the United States in 1641.

6. Was William Faulkner's *The Hamlet* (1940) favorably reviewed in *The New Yorker?*

7. What book, published in 1953, contains biographical information about Isadora Duncan?

Name _____ Date _____

8. Cite the title of a book *in the library* which includes the text of William Wycherley's play "The Country Wife," together with texts of plays by other authors.

_____

9. In what year was a movie made of Faulkner's novel *Intruder in the Dust?*

_____

10. Cite a historical novel whose setting is ancient Egypt.

_____

11. Cite a short story about life on other planets.

_____

12. What book *in the library* contains the short story "The Catbird Seat"?

_____

13. Cite a book published in 1958 which contains an essay about the philosopher David Hume.

_____

14. Where is the periodical *Werkstattstechnik* published?

_____

15. Cite the title of one source of statistics of automobile accidents in the United States.

_____

Name _____ Date _____

# 6.51
# The Bibliography Collection [Dewey]

Answer briefly the following questions. Since the bibliographies which you must consult will probably be scattered throughout the collection (instead of being grouped in one place, as they are in the Library of Congress system), you may need to use the subject catalog to locate some or all of them.

**Time: 2 hours**

1. Who is the author of the anonymously published work entitled *Fumifugium; or The Inconvenience of the Aer, and Smoake of London Dissipated; Together with Remedies Humbly Proposed* (1661)?

 

2. Cite one book published in the United States in 1641.

 

3. Was William Faulkner's *The Hamlet* (1940) favorably reviewed in *The New Yorker?*

 

4. What book, published in 1953, contains biographical information about Isadora Duncan?

 

5. Cite the title of a book *in the library* which includes the text of William Wycherley's play "The Country Wife," together with texts of plays by other authors.

 

Name_____Date_____

6. What book *in the library* contains the short story "The Catbird Seat"?

_____

7. Cite a book published in 1958 which contains an essay about the philosopher David Hume.

_____

8. Where is the periodical *Werkstattstechnik* published?

_____

# The Reference Collection

Answer briefly the following questions. First, indicate beside each question what *major* class in the reference collection (e.g. PN, PR, QA, QB, etc., or, in Dewey, 810, 820, 920, 930, etc.) should contain a book that will provide the answer. Then go to the shelves of the reference collection and attempt to locate the answers.

**Time: 1 hour**

1. When was the Book of Job written?

_____

2. Where is General Beadle State Teachers College located?

_____

3. Is the painter Joan Miró a man or a woman?

_____

4. In what kind of ground (according to his epitaph) was the great English printer John Baskerville buried?

_____

5. What is another name for the Greek god Hermes?

_____

6. What poem contains the line "Lo, the poor Indian"?

_____

7. What particular contribution did Kurt Gödel make to mathematical theory?

_____

Name_____Date_____

8. Cite one event in U.S. history that occurred in 1794.

_____

9. What is the height of Mount Olympus?

_____

10. Was U.S. Senator John Sherman Cooper a Democrat or a Republican in 1964?

_____

Name_____ Date_____

# 7

# The Catalog: Filing Problems

**Time: 1 hour**

A. Cite the title of one book in the catalog *by* each of the authors listed below:

1. Paul de Kruif

_____

2. Garcia Lorca

_____

3. Jean de la Bruyère

_____

4. Struthers Burt

_____

5. Rupert Hart-Davis

_____

6. Richard, Freiherr von Krafft-Ebing

_____

7. Ronald Firbank

_____

8. José Ortega y Gasset

_____

9. Saint Ignatius de Loyola

_____

Name_____ Date_____

10. Miguel de Cervantes Saavedra.

---

B. Cite the author *only* of one book entered in the subject catalog under each of the following headings:

1. Göring, Hermann

---

2. United States. Navy

---

3. United States—History—Civil War

---

4. United States—History—Colonial period

---

5. United States—History, Military

---

6. Art, Abstract

---

7. Art—France

---

8. Philosophy, Ancient

---

9. Philosophy and religion

---

10. Philosophy—History

---

Name_____ Date_____

# Exercise
# 8
# Corporate-Name Entries

Cite the *short title* of one entry in the catalog (author-title or subject, as appropriate) that answers each of the following descriptions.

**Time: 1 hour**

1. A copy of the Bill of Rights.

_____

2. A book about the Bill of Rights.

_____

3. A book about the Nazi Party.

_____

4. A book about East Germany.

_____

5. A copy of the U. S. Census.

_____

6. A publication of the President's Science Advisory Committee.

_____

7. A publication of The New York Graphic Society.

_____

8. A book about the New York Metropolitan Opera.

_____

9. A book about the F.B.I.

_____

Name _____ Date_____

10. A book about the Peace Corps.

---

11. A publication of the University of Illinois.

---

12. A publication of the Board of Governors of the Federal Reserve System.

---

13. A book about the Eighteenth Amendment to the American Constitution.

---

14. A book about the Continental Congress.

---

15. A copy of the Declaration of Independence.

---

16. A copy of the prayer book of the Episcopal Church in the U.S.

---

17. A book about the Communist Party of Russia.

---

18. A publication of the Library of Congress.

---

19. A book about the Russian Army.

---

20. A book about the Securities and Exchange Commission.

---

Name_____ Date_____

# Government Documents:
# The Monthly Catalog

Listed below are descriptions of various U.S. government documents. Locate each document in the *Monthly Catalog* for 1970 or 1971 and list for each the following information: issuing department or agency, author (if given), brief title, edition, date, pages, price and Superintendent of Documents classification.

**Time: 1 hour**

1. Fish kills due to pollution.

_____

_____

2. A teacher's manual on what drugs do.

_____

_____

3. A consumers' guide on eggs in family meals.

_____

_____

4. Hearings on the role of studded tires in traffic safety.

_____

_____

5. Annual report of the Federal Power Commission.

_____

_____

Name_____ Date_____

6. A conference concerning pollution of Lake Superior.

_____

_____

7. A marine weather services chart from Eastport, Maine to Montauk Point, N.Y.

_____

_____

8. A 1970 census of population report on Vermont.

_____

_____

9. Hearings on the problems of Alaska.

_____

_____

10. Hearings on riots, civil and criminal disorders.

_____

_____

11. Documents relating to war powers of Congress.

_____

_____

12. A paper concerning ground water in Alaska.

_____

_____

13. A description and listing of tropical cyclones that have affected North Carolina.

_____

_____

14. A directory of Spanish-speaking organizations in the U.S.

_____

_____

Name_____ Date_____

Which monthly issue of the *Monthly Catalog* always lists depository libraries? Find the most recent one and name four depository libraries in your home state. Also name the regional depository library closest to your college or university.

_____

_____

_____

_____

_____

Does your library catalog all the government documents it acquires? If not, how does it record document holdings?

Name_____ Date_____

*Exercise*
# 9.2

# Government Documents: Congressional Information

Using the *Congressional Record* (bound volumes), the *Congressional Index, Congressional Directory,* and the *Monthly Catalog,* find the following information:

**Time: 2 hours**

1. Locate President Lyndon Johnson's message on Civil Rights (H. doc. 243) in the *Congressional Record,* 90th Congress, 2d session. Was this message printed more than once in the *Congressional Record?* State date of message.

---

2. a.   In one reference source, find the following data for a senator from your home state:   Brief biography, home address, Congressional address, list of committees and subcommittees on which he serves.

Name_____Date_____

b.  Find the same data for a representative from your home state.

3. Locate Senate Bill 976 of the 92nd Congress and give its brief title. List the co-sponsors of this bill. Give the dates of the Senate hearings on this bill, when it was reported, if and when amended, and latest status. Is there a companion bill to S. 976? If so, list it. Record the Senate vote(s) on this bill.

Name _____ Date _____

4. List the bills introduced in the 92nd Congress, 2nd Session by a representative from your home state. Give brief subject and bill number for each, as well as the representative's name.

5. a.  Give the political alignment of the U.S. Senate for the 92nd Congress, 2nd Session.

_____

   b.  Give the political alignment of the U.S. House of Representatives for the 92nd Congress, 2nd Session.

_____

6. Who is the present chairman of the House Education and Labor Committee? How many Democrats serve on this committee? How many Republicans serve on this committee? What is the jurisdiction of this committee? List all of the subcommittees of the House Education and Labor Committee.

Name _____ Date _____

7. Who is the current chairman of the Senate Armed Services Committee? How many Democrats and how many Republicans serve on this committee? What is the jurisdiction of this committee? List all the subcommittees of the Senate Armed Services Committee.

8. Give the bill number, short title, and approval date for each of the following public laws:

P. L.  92-14 _____

P. L.  92-31 _____

P. L.  92-39 _____

P. L.  92-50 _____

P. L.  92-65 _____

9. Find a bill sponsored by a congressman from your home state. Give its short title and trace its passage through Congress.

Name _____      Date _____

10. Locate biographical material for a congressman from your state in the latest edition of the *Congressional Directory* and compare this with the data given in the *Congressional Index*. What material do you find in the *Congressional Directory* which is not given in the *Congressional Index?* Which source provides more complete information on Washington residences and phone numbers?

11. Find the address of the following independent agencies and list the top official for each.

     a.   U.S. Arms Control and Disarmament Agency

     _____

     b.   U.S. Atomic Energy Commission

     _____

     c.   Civil Aeronautics Board

     _____

     d.   Export-Import Bank of the U.S.

     _____

     e.   Farm Credit Administration.

_____

12. On what page of the *Congressional Directory* do you find a map showing the congressional districts of your home state? Give your congressional district number.

_____

Name _____ Date _____

13. What hearing was held in New York City on Dec. 8, 1969 with Ralph
    Nader testifying? Cite the pages covering this in the *Congressional
    Record* for the 91st Congress, 2d Session. Describe entries listed under
    Ralph Nader in the index to

    a.  *Congressional Record,* v. 115 (91st Cong., 1st Sess.)
    b.  *Congressional Record,* v. 114 (90th Cong., 2d Sess.)

    Can an index entry be found in the *Monthly Catalog* under Nader's
    name?

Name_____ Date_____

*Exercise*
# 9.3
# Government Documents:
# The National Atlas

**Time: 1 hour**

1. On what pages do you find information on types and size of farms and farm labor?

_____

2. What types of economic activity are indicated on the map of national business centers?

_____

_____

3. What state led in wheat production in 1964?

_____

What states sold the most field crops in 1964?

_____

_____

List the leading states in corn harvested in 1964:

_____

_____

4. Find a chart giving average annual value of mineral products for the individual states and list the information given for your home state. What page had this data?

_____

_____

_____

Name_____ Date_____

5. a.  What two states lead in textile production?

_____

  b.  What state has the highest number of employees in tobacco production?

_____

  c.  What is the leading state for lumber and wood products?

_____

  d.  How many workers are employed in the leather and leather products industry in the state leading in this?

_____

6. What state had the greatest non-white population change between 1940-1960?

_____

  What was the increase?

_____

7. List the maps dealing with family income.

_____
_____
_____
_____
_____

8. List two Indian reservations, two national monuments, and two national wild-life refuges found on the Federal Lands map.

_____
_____
_____
_____
_____

9. Locate your home congressional district and list it. Also list the number of representatives for your home state.

_____
_____

Name _____ Date _____

10. Name your home state _____
    and give the following data for it:

      a. area in square miles:    land _____
                                      water _____
                                      total _____
                                      rank _____
      b. highest point:           name _____
                                      elevation (feet) _____
      c. lowest point:            name _____
                                      elevation (feet) _____
      d. geographic center: _____

11. a.  Name the longest river in the U.S.A.

_____

    b.  Name the highest peak.

_____

    c.  Name the largest lake.

_____

    d.  Name the highest waterfall.

_____

Name _____ Date _____

*Exercise*
# 9.4
# Government Documents:
# Public Affairs Information Service

Using recent annual cumulated volumes of *PAIS,* locate and list one of each of the following types of publications for each subject listed below: (1) a state document, (2) a Congressional hearing or other government document, (3) a bibliography, (4) a book.

**Time: 1 hour**

1. Environment

_____
_____
_____
_____

2. Urban redevelopment

_____
_____
_____
_____

3. Juvenile delinquency

_____
_____
_____
_____

4. Conservation

_____
_____

Name _____ Date _____

_____

_____

5. Political campaigns

_____

_____

_____

_____

6. Child welfare

_____

_____

_____

_____

7. Political activities of college students

_____

_____

_____

_____

8. Drug abuse

_____

_____

_____

_____

9. Rapid transit

_____

_____

_____

_____

10. Minorities

_____

_____

_____

_____

Name_____ Date_____

*Exercise*
# 9.5
# Government Documents: Bibliographies

Using the *Monthly Catalog* (1970 and 1971), locate a bibliography on each subject and list full title, date, number of pages, price, and Superintendent of Documents number.

**Time: 15 minutes**

1. Arms control and disarmament.

_____

_____

_____

2. Communist China.

_____

_____

_____

3. Drug dependence and abuse.

_____

_____

_____

4. Crime and delinquency.

_____

_____

_____

5. Folklore of North American Indians.

_____

_____

_____

Name_____Date_____

In the *Monthly Checklist of State Publications* (1971), find the following items and cite entry number, issuing department, full title, date, number of pages, and price (if given).

**Time: 15 minutes**

1. Florida official road map.

_____

_____

_____

2. Angler's guide to Lake Tahoe (Nevada).

_____

_____

_____

3. Vocational programs for the disadvantaged in Maine.

_____

_____

_____

4. Alcoholic beverage control laws of Mississippi.

_____

_____

_____

5. Statistical report on mental hospitals in Kentucky.

_____

_____

_____

Name_____ Date_____

## *Exercise*
# 9.6

# Government Documents: Census Publications

Using the *Catalog of U. S. Census Publications, 1790-1945,* locate the following publications and cite both the entry and Superintendent of Documents number.

**Time: 15 minutes**

1. The census listing heads of families at the first U. S. census.

_____
_____
_____

2. An abstract of the Fifth Census which shows the number of free people and the number of slaves.

_____
_____
_____

3. Manufactures of the U. S. in 1860.

_____
_____
_____

4. A 1943 report on abandoned or idle farms.

_____
_____
_____

5. Census of religious bodies in 1926.

_____
_____
_____

Name_____ Date_____

Using the *Bureau of the Census Catalog* for 1970 and 1971, locate the following publications, and cite both entry and Superintendent of Documents number.

**Time: 15 minutes**

1. The state-county subdivision map for your home state.

_____

_____

_____

2. A report on local government employment in selected metropolitan areas and large counties.

_____

_____

_____

3. A publication on poverty increases in 1970.

_____

_____

_____

4. A 1970 census of population report on the number of inhabitants of your home state.

_____

_____

_____

5. A publication on the changing characteristics of the Negro population.

_____

_____

_____

Name _____ Date _____

# *Exercise*
# 10
# The Strategy of Search

**Time: 3 hours**

A. What would be the *best* way to locate, compile, or determine the following?

1. The age at which Shakespeare married.

_____

2. A recent scholarly essay on American foreign relations.

_____

3. A list of books owned by the Library of Congress.

_____

4. All dictionaries and encyclopedias of the Bible owned by your library.

_____

5. A biographical sketch of a minor English political figure.

_____

6. The titles of several periodicals that your library owns in the field of education.

_____

7. A single book whose title you remember but whose author you have forgotten.

_____

8. A list of books published about Shakespeare in 1960.

_____

9. A bound volume of the *Journal of English and Germanic Philology.*

_____

Name _____ Date _____

10. A single book whose author and title you have forgotten.

_____

11. A list of all of Hemingway's books owned by your library.

_____

12. A comprehensive list of periodical articles, books, newspaper articles, essays, and poems about George Washington, whether owned by your library or not.

_____

13. The author who wrote "A foolish consistency is the hobgoblin of little minds."

_____


B. Choose a topic of suitable dimensions for a research paper of several thousand words (or whatever length your instructor may specify), and compile a complete preliminary bibliography for the paper, including reference books, bibliographies, periodical articles, essays, books, and anything else that is appropriate. Cite only publications that you have found in your library, making your citation from the work itself.

Name_____ Date_____